Contents

Relational Database Design

Introduction

A simple database consists of just one table of data. Each row in the table holds one record and each record has a primary key which uniquely identifies that record. This is known as a flat file database. For example Table 1.1 shows records of people going on various activity weekends.

FirstName	Surname	ContactName	ContactNo	DateOfBirth	Activity
John	Hainsworth	Mrs Hainsworth	01474 678456	26/5/89	Windsurf
Tony	Hodson	Mr Hodson	01474 212394	7/9/84	Abseil
Mike	Stevenson	Mr Denton	01474 665498	15/11/90	Abseil
Sharon	Hart	Mr Hart	01474 374509	22/4/85	Riding
Richard	Ellis	Mrs Muller	01474 151884	12/8/88	Windsurf
Lucie	Harris	Mrs Harris	01474 908635	14/12/90	Riding
Beccy	Lock	Mrs Lock	01474 505783	3/6/84	Windsurf
Omar	Iqbal	Mr Iqbal	01474 673028	5/7/91	Abseil
Gareth	Jones	Mr Jones	01474 255836	26/6/85	Windsurf
Seb	Harris	Mr Harris	01474 682453	21/6/86	Archery

Table 1.1

Problems with a flat file database

Now suppose that each activity costs a different amount and this information needs to be stored in the database. We could have an extra column in the table to store the cost. However if there were 20 people going windsurfing we would have to type in the cost of windsurfing 20 different times.

Also, suppose each member can do as many activities as they like. John Hainsworth might want to go windsurfing, abseiling and riding. This means there will have to be three records in the table for him and we will have to enter all his personal details (first name, surname, contact name, etc.) in all three records.

The table would then look like Table 1.2.

FirstName	Surname	ContactName	ContactNo	DateOfBirth	Activity	Activity Cost
John	Hainsworth	Mrs Hainsworth	01474 678456	26/5/89	Windsurf	25
John	Hainsworth	Mrs Hainsworth	01474 678456	26/5/89	Abseil	20
John	Hainsworth	Mrs Hainsworth	01474 678456	26/5/89	Riding	15
Tony	Hodson	Mr Hodson	01474 212394	7/9/84	Abseil	20
Mike	Stevenson	Mr Denton	01474 665498	15/11/90	Abseil	20
Sharon	Hart	Mr Hart	01474 374509	22/4/85	Riding	15
Richard	Ellis	Mrs Muller	01474 151884	12/8/88	Windsurf	25
Lucie	Harris	Mrs Harris	01474 908635	14/12/90	Riding	15
Beccy	Lock	Mrs Lock	01474 505783	3/6/84	Windsurf	25
Omar	Iqbal	Mr Iqbal	01474 673028	5/7/91	Abseil	20
Gareth	Jones	Mr Jones	01474 255836	26/6/85	Windsurf	25
Seb	Harris	Mr Harris	01474 682453	21/6/86	Archery	10

Table 1.2

This table has several problems. For one thing the personal data for John (first name, surname etc) has to be typed in three times, which is a waste of time. Secondly it would be easy to make a spelling mistake in the surname in one of the records.

FirstName	Surname	ContactName	ContactNo	DateOfBirth	Activity	Activity Cost
John	Hansworth	Mrs Hainsworth	01474 678456	26/5/89	Riding	15

Now if you wanted to look up all the records for John Hainsworth only two records would be found and John would miss out on the riding trip!

Thirdly, if John changed his telephone number (contact number) you would have to remember to change it in three different records, not just one.

A relational database

The solution to these problems is to hold the data in separate tables. We need a table for the people and a different table for the activities. The two tables will need to be linked. A database that contains more than one linked table is called a relational database. Before you learn how to design this sort of database you need to learn some new vocabulary.

Entity
An entity is a person or thing about which data is held. In our example there are two entities, Member and Activity.

Attribute
An attribute is a piece of information about the entity. For example the attributes belonging to the entity Member are first name, surname, contact name, contact no and date of birth.

Question: What attribute belongs to the entity Activity shown in Table 1.2?

Answer: Cost.

Relationships

There are three different types of relationship between entities.

One-to-one   e.g. Husband and wife. A husband can have one wife and a wife can have one husband.

One-to-many   e.g. Football team and player. A football team has many players, but a player belongs to only one team.

Many-to-many e.g. Student and subject. A student studies many subjects and a subject is studied by many students.

Question: Which of these relationships applies to Member and Activity in the example above?

Answer: Many-to-many: One member can take part in many activities, and one activity is done by many people.

Entity-relationship diagrams

Each of these relationships can be shown in an Entity-Relationship (E-R) diagram, as in Figure 1.3.

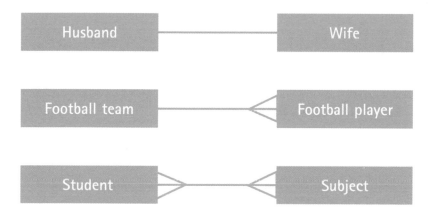

Figure 1.3: Entity-Relationship diagrams

Designing the database

Each entity needs its own table containing its own attributes. In addition each record in a table must have a field which uniquely identifies that record; this is called the primary key. Often there is no single field that is unique to each record; for example there may be two Hainsworths. In the activity table, the activity Riding may take place on several weekends, so referring to the activity Riding will not pinpoint which exact weekend is meant.

The solution is to add an extra field such as MemberID, ActivityID to each table to act as the primary key field. Now the two tables look like this:

Member table

MemberID	Surname	FirstName	DateOfBirth	ContactNo
M1	Hainsworth	John	26/5/89	01474 678456
M2	Hodson	Tony	7/9/84	01474 212394
M3	Hart	Sharon	22/4/85	01474 374509

Table 1.4: Member table

Activity table

ActivityID	Name	Date	Cost
A1	Riding	14/6/2001	15
A2	Windsurf	25/7/2001	25
A3	Abseil	5/6/2001	20

Table 1.5: Activity table

Linking the two tables

Hang on a minute! This is very neat but now we don't know who's going on which activity.

We need an extra table that lists who is going on which activity. This table only needs to contain MemberID and ActivityID, as shown in Table 1.6.

Member / Activity table

MemberID	ActivityID
M1	A1
M1	A2
M1	A3
M2	A2
M3	A3

Table 1.6: Member / Activity table

Question: Using Table 1.6 and the Member and Activity tables (Tables 1.4 and 1.5), can you list who is doing each activity?

Sometimes, a single field is not enough to uniquely identify a record. In Table 1.6 you would have to look at both fields to know which record you were in, so both fields form part of the primary key.

Now we have three tables in the database, linked as shown in Figure 1.7.

Figure 1.7: E-R diagram for the Activities database

Creating Tables

Crime database

We are going to create a database that is similar to that used in police stations, although of course it is a lot simpler.

It is important to plan a database before trying to implement it in Access – if the database design is wrong then your database won't work in the way you want. First you must be sure you understand the purpose of the database and what information the users (in this example, the police) want from it.

The police keep records of people who have committed crimes and whom they believe might commit another crime. When a new crime is reported they can search their database of suspects to see if anyone fits the description given by a witness, or if the crime is very similar to one that has been committed before.

The database will hold details of

 criminals, and the crimes they have committed

 unsolved crimes

There are two entities in this database about which information will be held: Criminal and Crime.

Relationships

Now let's think about the relationship between these entities. The following statements are true:

One crime may be committed by many criminals.

One criminal may have committed many crimes.

From these statements we can see that the relationship between crime and criminal is many-to-many.

The Entity-Relationship (E-R) diagram looks like this:

Figure 2.1

Whenever there is a many-to-many relationship, a third table is required in the middle to link the two tables.

For this database, the table 'in the middle' will contain information specifying who has committed which crime, and each record will contain CrimeID and CriminalID. The E-R diagram now looks like this:

Figure 2.2

Tip:
The extra table will always contain the key fields from each of the original two tables. Both these fields become key fields in the third table.

This may seem a little confusing, but if you find it difficult to see why the third table is required, you really can just try and remember this rule: wherever there is a many-to-many relationship, an extra table is required in the middle.

We now need to consider what information to hold about each entity.

For each criminal we will want to know name and address, as well as information such as date of birth, hair colour and height, which will help to identify them.

For each crime we'll need information such as crime type, date, area, and whether or not it has been solved.

Below is the formal way of writing which attributes belong to each entity.

CRIMINAL (CriminalID, Surname, FirstName, Sex, DOB, HairColour, Height, Area)

CRIME (CrimeID, CrimeType, Date, Time, Area, Solved)

The third table will be called SolvedCrimes and will look like this:

SOLVEDCRIMES (CrimeID, CriminalID)

Notice that in this table the primary key is a composite key consisting of two fields. This is because a particular record cannot be identified without knowing both fields. For example, if a criminal has committed many crimes, there will be several entries in this table for that criminal. If a crime involved several criminals, there will be several records with the same CrimeID.

Naming Conventions

The entity names in the database are Criminal, Crime and SolvedCrimes. Each entity will be the basis of a table. Recall that when naming tables you should put the letters tbl in front. The table names in the database will be tblCriminal, tblCrime and tblSolvedCrimes.

The field names in each table will be the same as the attribute names for each entity.

The tables are listed below along with all their attributes. These tables, along with the Entity-Relationship diagrams, are all you need to design the structure of your database.

tblCriminal

Field Name	Data Type	Field length/Type
CriminalID	Number	Long Integer
Surname	Text	30
FirstName	Text	20
Sex	Text	1
DOB	Date/Time	
HairColour	Text	15
Height	Number	Double
Area	Text	20

Figure 2.3

tblCrime

Field Name	Data Type	Field length/Type
CrimeID	Number	Long Integer
CrimeType	Text	20
Date	Date/Time	
Time	Date/Time	Short Time
Area	Text	20
Solved	Yes/No	Yes/No

Table 2.4

tblSolvedCrimes

Field Name	Data Type	Field Type
CrimeID	Number	Long Integer
CriminalID	Number	Long Integer

Table 2.5

You have learnt the basics of the database design – it's time to load up Access!

Loading Access

You can load Access in one of two ways:

Microsoft Access

▶ Either double-click the Access icon on the main screen in Windows

▶ or click the Start button at the bottom left of the screen, click Programs and select

 Microsoft Access

Your screen will look like Figure 2.6a if using Access 2000, 2.6b if using Access 2002 and 2.6c if using Access 2003:

Blank Database option

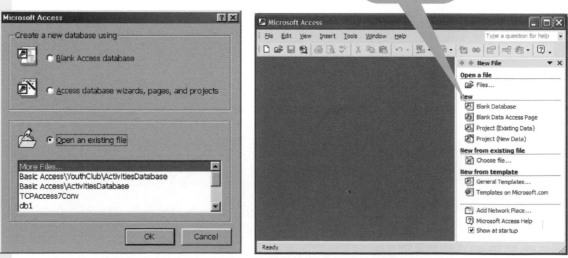

Figure 2.6a   *Figure 2.6b*

Opening screen Access 2000 (left) or Access 2002 (right)

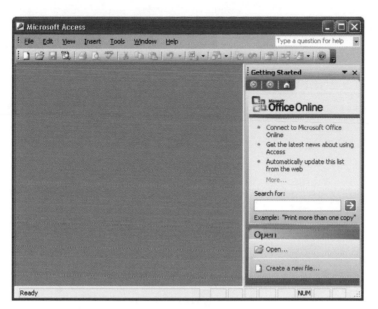

Figure 2.6c: Opening screen Access 2003

You now have the option of either opening an existing database or creating a new one. We will create a new database from scratch.

 In Access 2000 select the Blank Access Database button and press OK. In Access 2002 click Blank Database on the right hand pane. In Access 2003 click Create a new file in the right-hand pane, and then Blank database.

A window opens as shown in Figure 2.7, asking you to select a folder and a name for your new database.

 Click the Create New Folder button and create a new folder named Crime.

 In the File Name box, type the name CrimeDatabase (no spaces), and press the Create button. Access will automatically add the file extension .mdb.

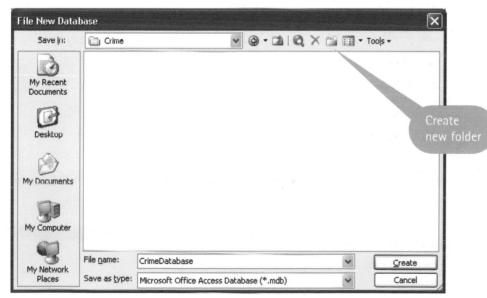

Figure 2.7: Saving a new database

The database structure

The tables, entities, attributes and relationships make up the database structure. We will now build the database structure in Access.

The Database window

Access databases are made up of objects. A table is an object, and is the only object we have talked about so far. Other objects which you will come across in this book include Queries, Forms and Reports.

The Database window is a sort of central menu from which you can open or create these objects. The window has buttons for each type of database object such as Tables, Queries, Forms or Reports.

Tables is currently selected, and since at the moment there are no existing tables to Open or Design, only the Create options are active.

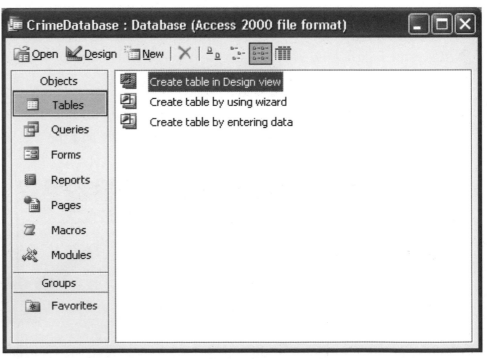

Figure 2.8: The Database window

Creating a new table

 In the Database window make sure the Tables button is selected, and press New.

A New Table window appears.

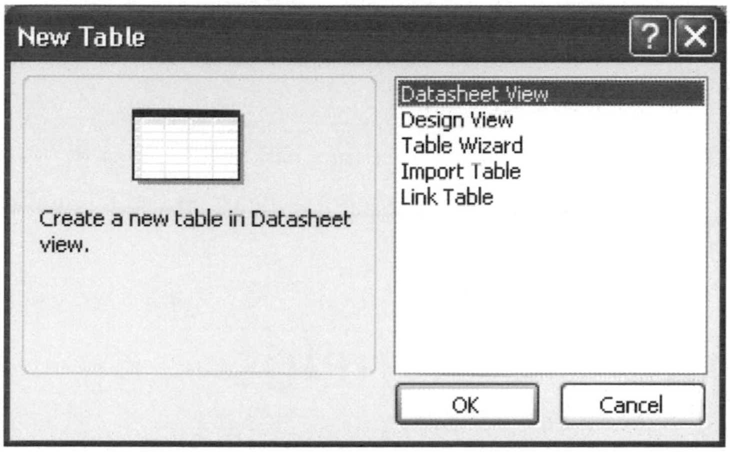

Figure 2.9: Creating a new table

 Select Design View and click OK.

The Table Design window appears.

Look back at the structure of the tblCriminal table in Table 2.3. All these fields need to be entered in the new table.

 Enter the first field name, CriminalID, and tab to the Data Type column.

 Click the down arrow and select the field type Number.

 Tab to the Description column and type This is the Key field.

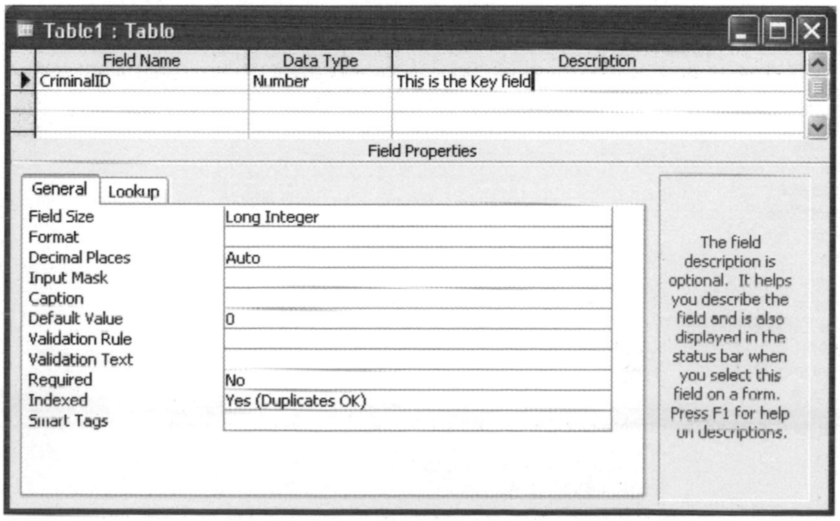

Figure 2.10

Tip:

There are several different sorts of **Number** field. You can see them by clicking the down arrow next to **Field Size** under **Field Properties**. Leave this **Number** field as **Long Integer**.

Defining the primary key

Every table in an Access database must have a primary key (also known as the key field). The field which you specify for the primary key must have a different value for each record. For tblCriminal we will define CriminalID as the primary key. We cannot use Surname because there may be more than one criminal with the same surname.

 With the cursor still in the row for CriminalID, press the Primary Key icon on the toolbar. The key symbol appears in the left hand margin next to CriminalID.

Entering other fields

Now you can enter all the other fields.

 In the next row, enter the field name Surname and leave the data type in the next column as Text.

 In the bottom half of the window under Field Properties change the field length from 50 to 30.

 Enter the fields for FirstName and Sex. All these fields have a data type Text. Give each text field the correct length according to Table 2.3.

Field Name	Data Type	Description
CriminalID	Number	This is the Key field
Surname	Text	
FirstName	Text	
Sex	Text	

Field Properties

General | Lookup

Field Size	1
Format	
Input Mask	
Caption	
Default Value	
Validation Rule	
Validation Text	
Required	No
Allow Zero Length	Yes
Indexed	No
Unicode Compression	Yes
IME Mode	No Control
IME Sentence Mode	None
Smart Tags	

The data type determines the kind of values that users can store in the field. Press F1 for help on data types.

Figure 2.11

▶ Enter the field name DOB and give it a data type of Date/Time.

▶ Enter the field name HairColour and leave the data type as Text. Give it a field length of 15.

▶ Enter the field name Height and give it the data type Number.

▶ In the Field Properties, change the Field Size to Double.

▶ In the Description column type Height in metres.

▶ Enter the field name Area and give it the data type Text. Give it a field length of 20.

▶ Check that you've entered the correct field lengths from Table 2.3.

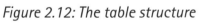

Tip:

Specifying **Double** will allow you to enter a number with a decimal place.

Your table should now look like Figure 2.12.

Field Name	Data Type	Description
⚷ CriminalID	Number	This is the Key field
Surname	Text	
FirstName	Text	
Sex	Text	
DOB	Date/Time	
HairColour	Text	
Height	Number	Height in metres
▶ Area	Text	

Field Properties

General	Lookup	
Field Size	20	
Format		
Input Mask		
Caption		
Default Value		
Validation Rule		
Validation Text		
Required	No	The data type determines the kind of values that users can store in the field. Press F1 for help on data types.
Allow Zero Length	Yes	
Indexed	No	
Unicode Compression	Yes	
IME Mode	No Control	
IME Sentence Mode	None	
Smart Tags		

Figure 2.12: The table structure

Saving the table

 Save the table by pressing the Save icon or selecting File, Save from the menu bar.

 You will be asked to type a name for your table. Type the name tblCriminal and click OK.

Validation

You can set limits on what a user is allowed to enter into any field, and specify a message which will be displayed if something different is entered. This is called data validation, and helps to make sure that the data entered is accurate.

First of all you have to decide which fields can be sensibly validated. For example, you may decide that:

 the CriminalID field must consist of only digits 0-9.

 Surname and FirstName fields cannot be left blank.

 the field for Sex can only be either M or F.

the Height field must be between 1.0 and 2.5 metres.

Some validation is performed automatically by Access – for example, it will be impossible to enter anything except numbers into a field which has the data type Number. Similarly, it will be impossible to enter an invalid date such as 25/13/2001 into a field with data type Date/Time.

Some fields are almost impossible for a computer to validate. For example a surname or first name could contain different characters such as - or ' as well as letters, and no validation rule will pick out a misspelt name.

Making data entry mandatory

First of all, we will make sure the user enters something in the Surname and FirstName fields.

 Click in the Surname field.

 In the Field Properties set Required to Yes.

Do the same for the FirstName field.

Allowing only certain values

 Click in the field for Sex.

 In the Validation Rule property, type M or F.

 In the Validation Text property, type Sex must be M or F. This is the message that will be displayed if the user enters anything else in this field.

Allowing a range of values

 Click in the Height field. Suppose you decide that the range of valid heights is between 1m and 2.5m.

 In the Validation Rule property, type Between 1.0 and 2.5.

 In the Validation Text property, type Height must be between 1 and 2.5 metres.

	Field Name	Data Type	Description
🔑	CriminalID	Number	This is the Key field
	Surname	Text	
	FirstName	Text	
	Sex	Text	
	DOB	Date/Time	
	HairColour	Text	
▶	Height	Number	Height in metres
	Area	Text	

Field Properties

General | Lookup

Field Size	Double
Format	
Decimal Places	Auto
Input Mask	
Caption	
Default Value	0
Validation Rule	Between 1 And 2.5
Validation Text	Height must be between 1 and 2.5 metres
Required	No
Indexed	No
Smart Tags	

The error message that appears when you enter a value prohibited by the validation rule. Press F1 for help on validation text.

Figure 2.13: Setting validation rules and text

 Save the table again.

Testing your validation rules

The next thing is to see what happens when a user tries to enter invalid data.

Click the View button on the toolbar to change to Datasheet View. In this view you can enter some test data.

Enter a Surname and FirstName as in Figure 2.14. In the Sex field, enter an invalid letter such as q. You will see the error message appear as soon as you tab out of the field, and you will not be allowed to continue until you enter a valid value.

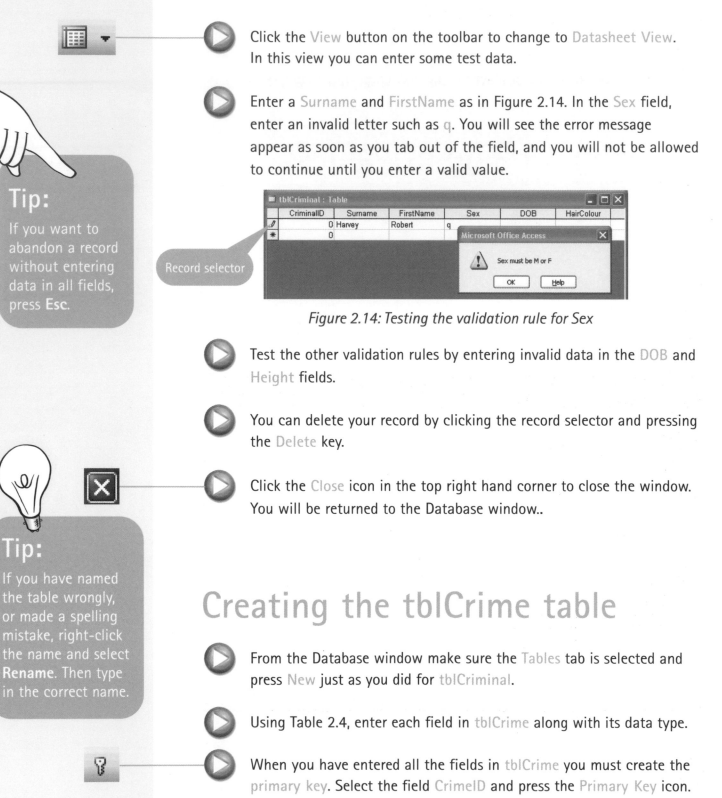

Figure 2.14: Testing the validation rule for Sex

Test the other validation rules by entering invalid data in the DOB and Height fields.

You can delete your record by clicking the record selector and pressing the Delete key.

Click the Close icon in the top right hand corner to close the window. You will be returned to the Database window..

Creating the tblCrime table

From the Database window make sure the Tables tab is selected and press New just as you did for tblCriminal.

Using Table 2.4, enter each field in tblCrime along with its data type.

When you have entered all the fields in tblCrime you must create the primary key. Select the field CrimeID and press the Primary Key icon.

Remember to enter the correct field lengths and formats in the Field Properties (look at Table 2.4).

Save the table as tblCrime and then close it.

Creating a composite key field

Create a third new table for tblSolvedCrimes.

Enter the field names and types using Table 2.5.
This table has a primary key which consists of both fields. To define the primary key:

 Using the mouse, highlight the two fields CrimeID and CriminalID in the table, by clicking one row selector and dragging down to the other.

 Press the Primary Key icon on the toolbar.

Tip:
The row selectors are the small grey boxes to the left of the **Field Name** box.

Table1 : Table

	Field Name	Data Type	Description
🔑	CrimeID	Number	
🔑▶	CriminalID	Number ▾	

Field Properties

General | Lookup

Field Size	Long Integer
Format	
Decimal Places	Auto
Input Mask	
Caption	
Default Value	0
Validation Rule	
Validation Text	
Required	No
Indexed	Yes (Duplicates OK)
Smart Tags	

The data type determines the kind of values that users can store in the field. Press F1 for help on data types.

Row selector

Figure 2.15

 Save the table as tblSolvedCrimes and then close it.

 Close your database by selecting File, Close from the menu bar and saving changes if prompted.

ST. MARY'S UNIVERSITY COLLEGE
A COLLEGE OF THE QUEEN'S UNIVERSITY OF BELFAST

Setting up Relationships

Opening an existing database

▶ Load Access. One of the following windows will appear.

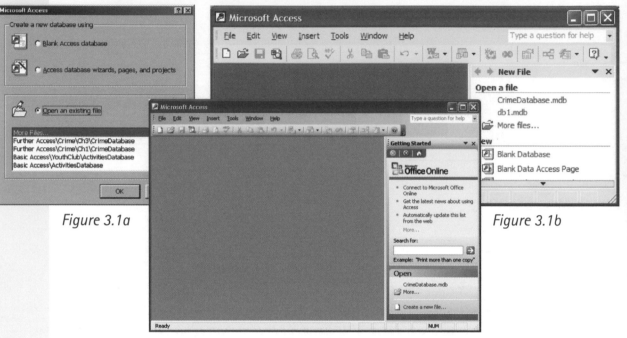

Figure 3.1a

Figure 3.1b

Figure 3.1c
Opening an existing database in 2000, 2002 or 2003

 In Access 2000, select Open an existing file, then find the file CrimeDatabase in the box below. It should be in a folder named Crime. Click OK.

 In Access 2002 or 2003 click the file CrimeDatabase.mdb from the list on the right hand pane.

The Database window will appear.

In the first chapter we looked at the relationships between the tables, and drew entity-relationship diagrams to represent them. Now that the tables have been created we must link them in Access.

Relationships window

 On the main toolbar, click Tools, Relationships.

The Show Table window will appear:

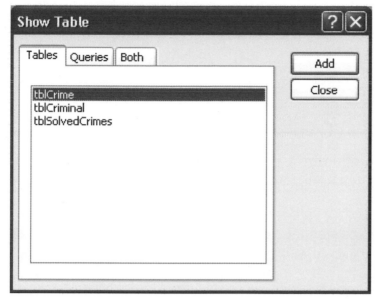

Figure 3.2

We want to form relationships between all three tables, so we will want all tables to appear in the Relationships window.

 Highlight each one in turn, keeping your finger on the Ctrl key, and click Add.

 Click Close.

All three tables should now be in the Relationships window as shown in Figure 3.3:

Figure 3.3

Tip:
If this window does not appear, select **View, Show Table**.

Rearranging the tables

Before creating the relationships it is convenient to rearrange the tables to match the E-R diagram. In this case tblSolvedCrimes needs to be between tblCrime and tblCriminal.

 Move the tables by clicking and dragging the blue bar at the top of each table.

Creating a relationship

Recall from Chapter 1 that there is a one-to-many relationship between tblCrime and tblSolvedCrimes.

 Click and drag the field CrimeID from tblCrime and drop it onto the field CrimeID in tblSolvedCrimes.

 The Edit Relationships window will appear:

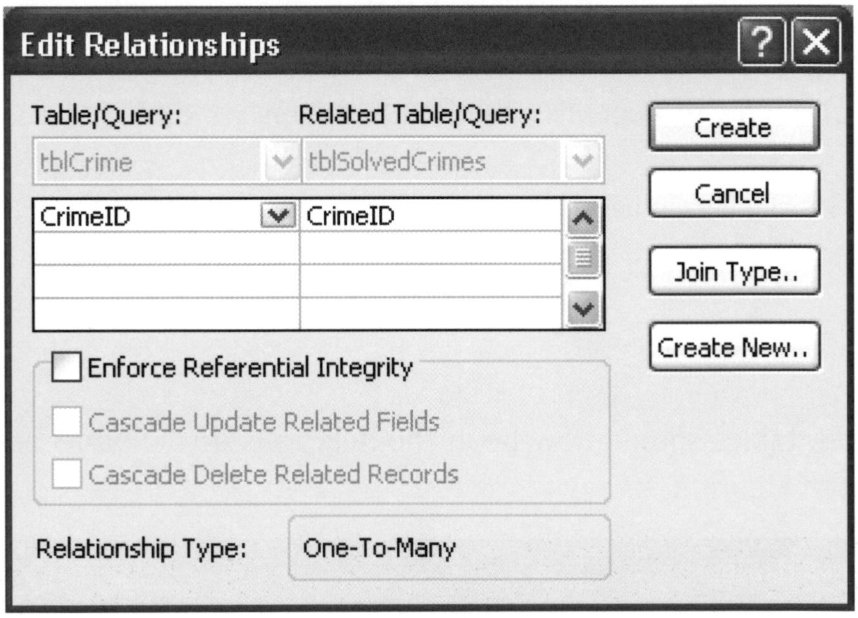

Edit Relationships

Table/Query:	Related Table/Query:
tblCrime	tblSolvedCrimes

CrimeID	CrimeID

☐ Enforce Referential Integrity

☐ Cascade Update Related Fields

☐ Cascade Delete Related Records

Relationship Type: One-To-Many

Create
Cancel
Join Type..
Create New..

Figure 3.4

 Click the box marked Enforce Referential Integrity to select it, then press Create.

You have now created a relationship between those two tables. Now you have to do the same for the other relationship:

Click and drag the field CriminalID from tblCriminal and drop it onto the field CriminalID in tblSolvedCrimes.

Again, the Edit Relationships window appears.

 Click Enforce Referential Integrity, then click Create.

The Relationships window should now look like Figure 3.5:

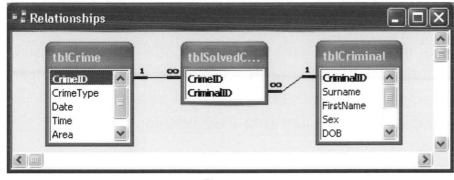

Figure 3.5

Don't worry if your window doesn't look like this – you can follow the instructions below to edit the relationships.

Deleting relationships

It's easy to delete or edit a relationship. Suppose you want to delete a relationship:

 Click on the relationship (represented by a line) between tblCrime and tblSolvedCrimes.

The line becomes bold to show that it is selected.

 Press the Delete key.

The following message will appear:

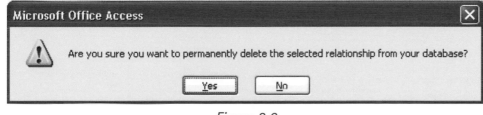

Figure 3.6

 Click Yes.

Tip:

Check to see that the relationships are the right way round - if they're not, you probably dragged the fields **from** instead of **to** tblSolvedCrimes.

Notice that the relationship has now been deleted.

Now change the relationships back so they look like they did in Figure 3.5. Note that to create a one-to-many relationship always drag from the one side of the relationship to the many side.

Word of warning!

When there is no data in the database it is very easy to edit the relationships. Once you have entered data, it will still be possible to edit the relationships but this is not advisable. If you change a relationship after data has been entered, Access may get confused, and you could find puzzling error messages appearing at inconvenient moments.

Saving the relationships

When you are satisfied that the relationships are correct, click the Close icon to return to the Database window. The relationships will automatically be saved, but you will be asked if you want to save the layout changes. Click Yes.

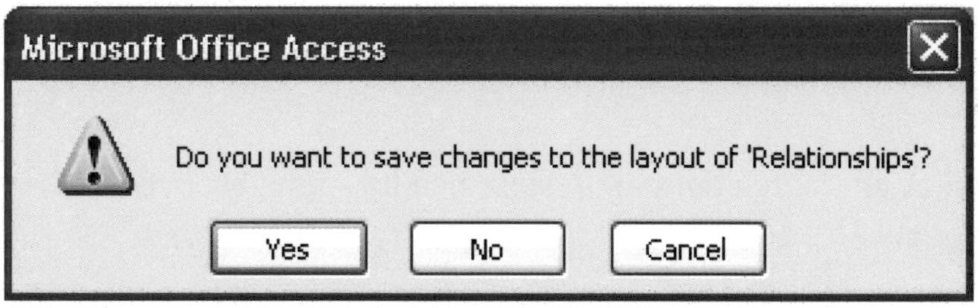

Figure 3.7

Forms and Command Buttons

User interface

You need to consider how the users interact with your computer application – how they choose what to do next, how they enter data and so on. You need to create an attractive user interface so that it is easy to enter data and to navigate around the various options.

We will start by creating a form to allow the user to input data about crimes.

This form will be used to log a crime once it has been reported.

Creating a new form

▶ Load up CrimeDatabase.

▶ In the Database window select the Forms button.

One of the options is to use a wizard. This is usually the quickest method, and the one you would normally use to create a simple form.

The only problem with wizards is that they do so much for you that it is sometimes difficult to see how to go back and change something. As a result people often start the whole form again if they have made a mistake in the form wizard – thus it can take longer than just learning how to create the form yourself!

For this reason we will not use a wizard this time, and you will see how easy it is to create the form yourself.

 Click New.

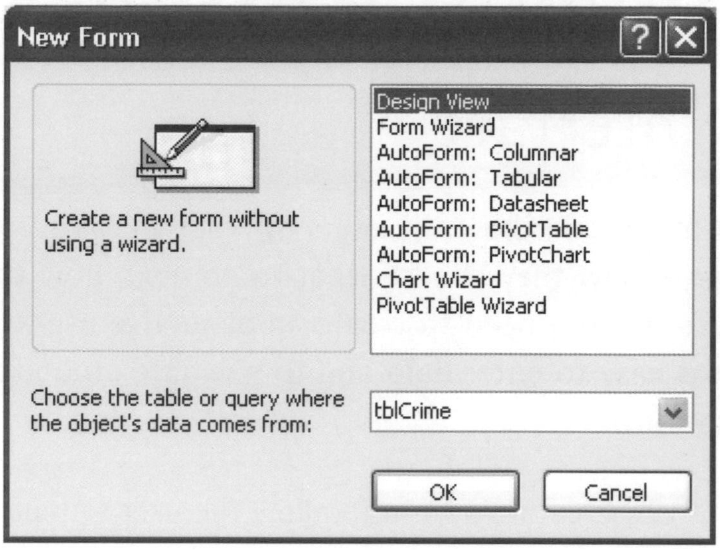

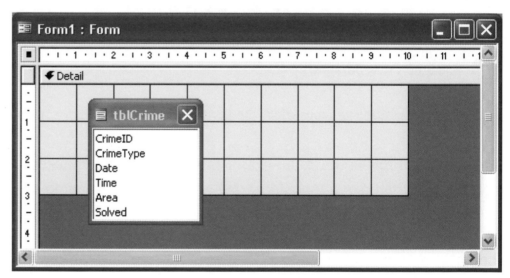

Figure 4.1: New Form window

 Design View should already be selected. In the drop-down list Choose the table or query..., select tblCrime. Click OK.

Figure 4.2

A blank form will appear along with the field list for tblCrime.

 If the field list does not appear, go to View, Field List.

 If the field list is blank, this will be because you didn't specify tblCrime from the drop-down list in the New Form window (Figure 4.1).

 To specify the table on which the form is based, right-click in the blue bar at the top of the form and select Properties from the menu that appears.

Figure 4.3: The Properties box

The Properties box appears.

 If you did select tblCrime in the first window, the row in the properties box marked Record Source will say tblCrime.

 If not, enter tblCrime as the Record Source.

 Close the Properties box by clicking its Close icon.

Now, with the field list in view, drag each field from tblCrime onto the blank form, so that it looks like Figure 4.4:

Figure 4.4

 Close the field list by clicking the Close icon.

Now save the form:

 Click the Save icon and enter frmCrime as the form name.

Tip:
You may want to experiment with the **Align**, **Horizontal Spacing** and **Vertical Spacing** option on the **Format** menu to tidy the form.

Form View

There are two views you can use to look at a form. Design View is the view you are in at the moment, and is used for editing the form. Form View is the view you would use if you were actually entering data.

▶ Click the Form View icon.

The form will now appear in Form View.

frmCrime : Form	— □ ✕
CrimeID:	`0`
CrimeType:	
Date:	
Time:	
Area:	☐ Solved

Record: |◀ ◀ 1 ▶ ▶| ▶✱ of 1

Figure 4.5: Form View

Modifying the form

There are two changes that can be made to the form to make data entry quicker and easier.

The first is to make some of the fields into list boxes. We will make the CrimeType field a list box so that you can pick CrimeType from a list instead of typing it in.

The second is to make the Date field automatically default to today's date. Since this form will be used to log crimes as they are reported, most crimes will be entered into the database on the day that they occur. If this is not the case, the date can be easily changed.

List Boxes

Return to Design View by clicking the Design View icon. ─────────────

Click the List Box icon in the Toolbox. ─────────────

Click about a field's width to the right of the CrimeType field, and drag out a rectangle.

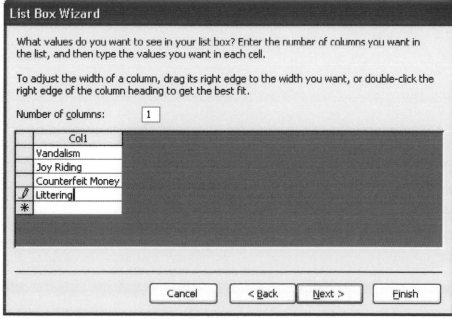

Figure 4.6: List Box Wizard

Select the middle option I will type in the values that I want. Click Next.

Leave the number of columns as 1. In the box below type in the crime types: Vandalism, Joy Riding, Counterfeit Money and Littering.

Figure 4.7

Tip:
Use the **Tab** key or the down arrow, *not* **Enter**, to move to the next entry.

Click Next. On the next page, select Store that value in this field and choose CrimeType as the field from the drop-down list. Click Next.

 Save the list box as CrimeType and click Finish.

You will notice that you now have two fields on your form for CrimeType. We need to delete the original CrimeType field.

 Click on the field to select it (make sure you click in the actual field, not its label). Press the Delete key.

 Now move the fields around until your form looks like Figure 4.8:

	frmCrime : Form		
CrimeID:	1	Date:	
Crime:	Vandalism Joy Riding Counterfeit Money Littering	Time:	
		Area:	
			☐ Solved

Record: |◄ ◄ 1 ► ►| ►* of 1

Figure 4.8: frmCrime in Form View

The Properties box

Every Control on a form (text box, list box, command button etc.) and even the form itself, has many properties which can be set. These include colour, font size, length, width, data source, default value and so on.

We will use the Properties box to change the default value of the date.

 In Design View, right-click on the Date field (not the label).

 Select Properties from the menu that appears.

 Select the Data tab at the top of the Properties box, and click in the row marked Default Value.

Text Box: Date

Date

| Format | Data | Event | Other | All |

Control Source . . . . Date
Input Mask . . . .
Default Value . . . .
Validation Rule . . . .
Validation Text . . . .
Enabled . . . . Yes
Locked . . . . No
Filter Lookup . . . . Database Default
Smart Tags . . . .

Figure 4.9: The Properties box

 Notice that a button appears on the right of the row. Press the ————————— [...] button.

The Expression Builder appears. This looks like a complicated box of tricks but it can be very useful.

 Press the = button in the Expression Builder.

 In the box on the left hand side, select Common Expressions from the bottom of the list.

In the middle box, you will see that Current Date has appeared as one of the options - along with other useful expressions which might be worth remembering for later use!

Expression Builder [?][X]

= Date() |

OK
Cancel
Undo

+ - / * & = > < <> And Or Not Like ( ) | Paste | Help

frmCrime	Page Number	Date()
Tables	Total Pages	
Queries	Page N of M	
Forms	Current Date	
Reports	Current Date/Time	
Functions	Current User	
Constants		
Operators		
Common Expressions		

Figure 4.10: The Expression Builder

 Double-click Current Date, and look in the top box to check that the expression now says = Date().

 Click OK.

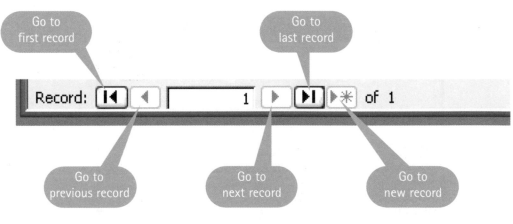

Figure 4.11

Close the Properties box by clicking the Close icon.

Press the Form View icon to see what the form will look like.

Command buttons

You are probably already familiar with the record selectors that appear at the bottom of the form (see Figure 4.12 for a reminder).

Go to first record

Go to last record

Record: ◄◄ ◄ 1 ► ►► ►* of 1

Go to previous record

Go to next record

Go to new record

Figure 4.12: The record selectors

A nicer way to move between records in a form is to create your own buttons.

You can create buttons to do a variety of tasks. We will make one that opens a blank form ready for data to be entered.

In Design View, click the Command Button icon in the Toolbox (next to the List Box icon).

 Click in an empty space on the form and drag out the shape you want for your button. (This can be adjusted later if you're not happy with it.)

The Command Button Wizard appears.

Figure 4.13: Command Button Wizard

 Have a look at the wide variety of things which the Command buttons can do by clicking in turn on the entries in the Categories list, and looking at the Actions that appear on the right.

 Now click on Record Operations in the Categories box and Add New Record in the Actions box.

 Click Next.

You are now asked to choose whether you want Text or a Picture to appear on the button.

 We want the button to say Log New Crime, so click in the box next to Text, and type Log New Crime.

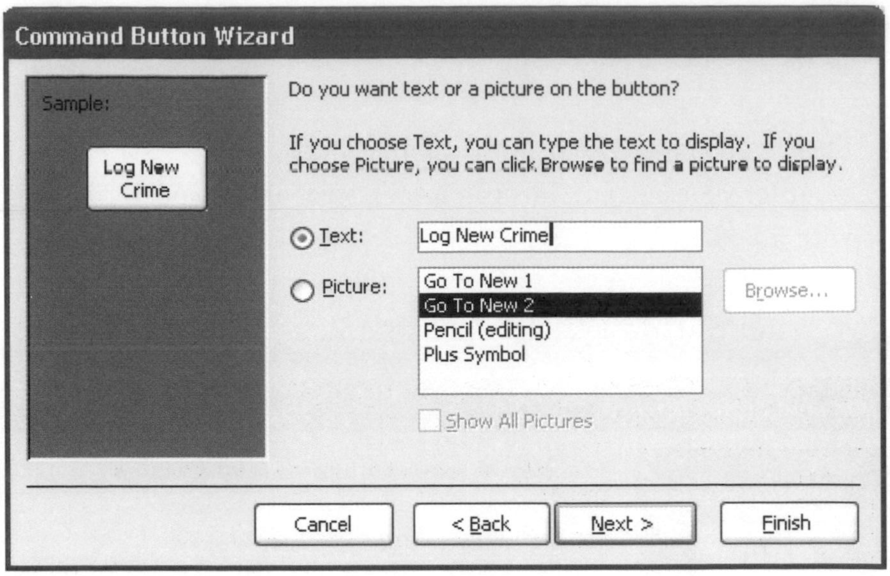

Command Button Wizard

Sample:

Log New Crime

Do you want text or a picture on the button?

If you choose Text, you can type the text to display. If you choose Picture, you can click Browse to find a picture to display.

- ⊙ Text: Log New Crime|
- ○ Picture: Go To New 1
  Go To New 2
  Pencil (editing)
  Plus Symbol

Browse...

☐ Show All Pictures

| Cancel | < Back | Next > | Finish |

Figure 4.14

▶ Click Next. Name the button NewCrimeButton and click Finish.

▶ Click the Form View icon. If you would like to change the shape of your button return to Design View and click and drag the corners of the button.

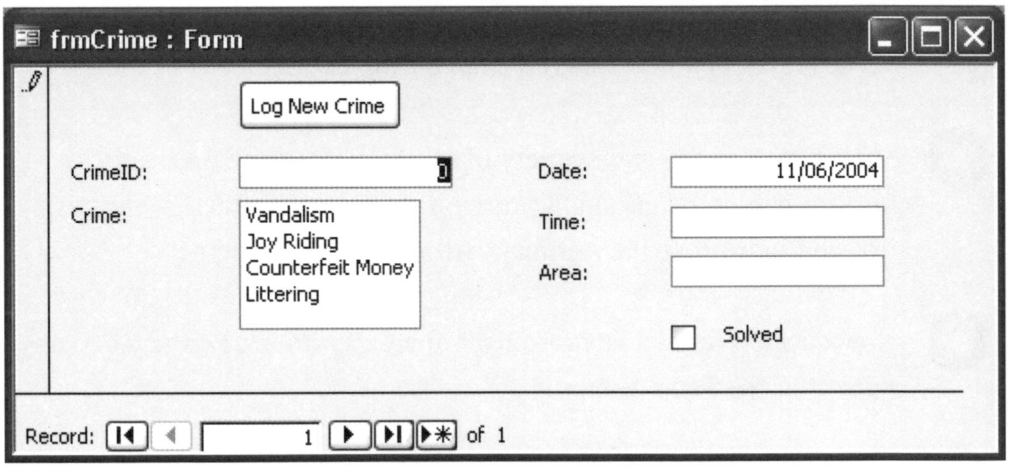

frmCrime : Form

Log New Crime

CrimeID: 0   Date: 11/06/2004

Crime: Vandalism   Time:
           Joy Riding
           Counterfeit Money   Area:
           Littering

☐ Solved

Record: ◀◀ ◀ | 1 | ▶ ▶▶ ▶* of 1

Figure 4.15

▶ When you are happy with the design, save and close the form.

Forms and Subforms

When this database is first installed, the first thing to do will be to type in existing data about criminals and the crimes they have committed. If you were typing in information on a criminal who had committed many crimes, it would be convenient to type in all the information about the criminal and the crimes on the same form. To do this you need a form with a subform.

Subforms

Subforms are basically forms within forms. They are used when there is a one-to-many relationship.

In databases with a one-to-many relationship, the fields from the table on the one side would be on the main form, and the fields from the many side would appear on the subform.

Taking the example of the football team and player as the one-to-many relationship:

You would have the football team on the main form, and within that would be a subform listing all the players within that team.

In this database we have 2 one-to-many relationships:

1. between tblCriminal and tblSolvedCrimes;

2. between tblCrime and tblSolvedCrimes.

We have two options:

1. Criminal could appear on the main form and the subform would contain all the crimes committed by that criminal;

2. Crime could appear on the main form and the subform would list all the criminals who were involved in that particular crime.

Of course we could have both types of form – we don't have to choose one!

We will create a form that fits the first option.

Creating the form

 In the Database window, make sure the Forms tab is selected and click New.

Figure 5.1: New Form window

 Select Form Wizard from the list that appears and click OK.

 In the Form Wizard window select Table: tblCriminal from the drop-down list.

We want all the fields in tblCriminal to appear on the main form so click >>.

 Now select Table: tblSolvedCrimes from the drop-down list.

We only want the field CrimeID from this table.

- Select CrimeID and click >.

>

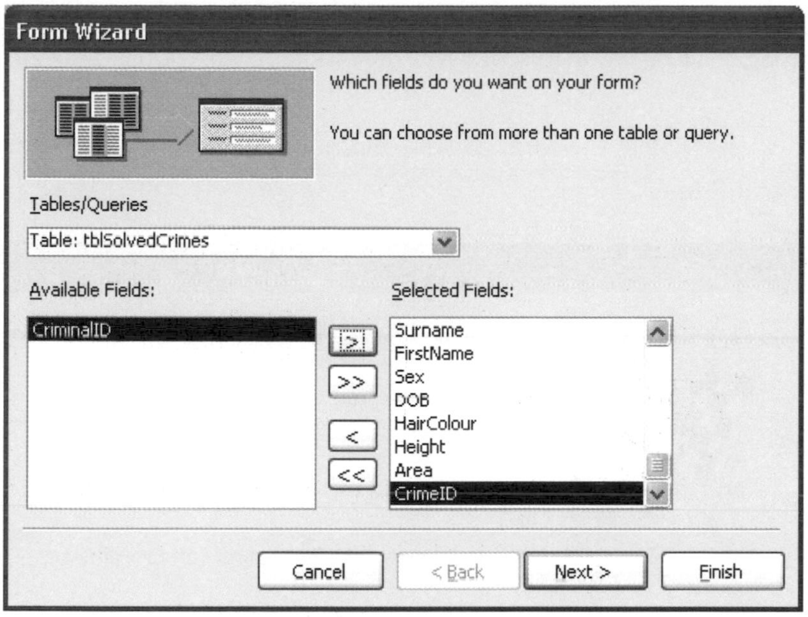

Figure 5.2: Form Wizard

- Now select Table: tblCrime from the drop-down list.
- Select the fields CrimeType, Date and Solved from tblCrime.
- Click Next.

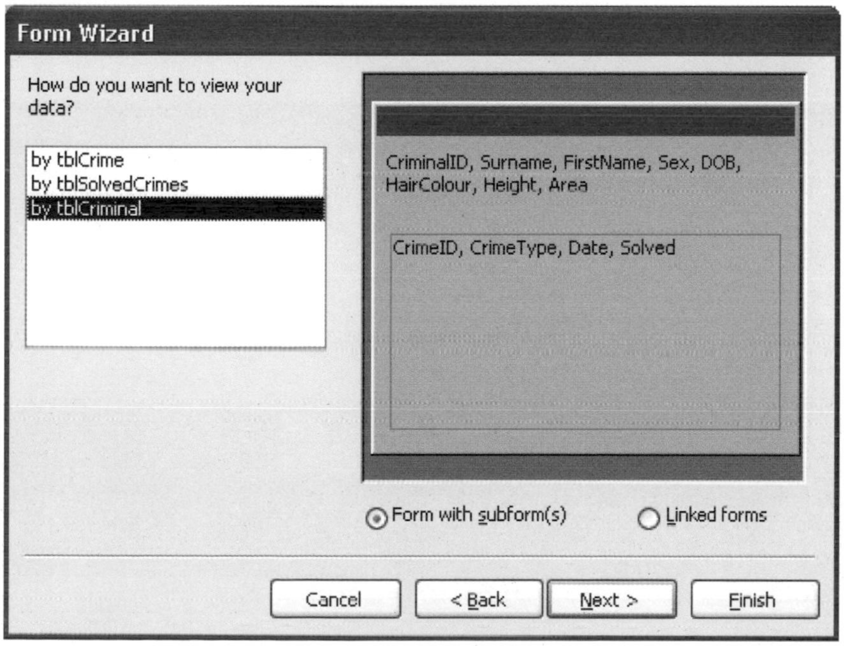

Figure 5.3

- Access now gives two options: to have either Crime or Criminal on the main form. We want Criminal to be on the main form, so make sure tblCriminal is selected in the box on the left.

Note:

It is important that **CrimeID** is taken from **tblSolvedCrimes** and not **tblCrime**. This is because **tblSolvedCrimes** is the table that links the criminal with the crimes he or she has committed. Details of these crimes can be looked up from **tblCrime**.

We are also given the option of Form with subform(s) or Linked forms. Make sure Form with subform(s) is selected and click Next.

 Select Datasheet from the next window and click Next.

Take a look at the different styles available, then choose Standard.

Click Next. Save the form as frmCriminalAndCrime and the subform as fsubCrime.

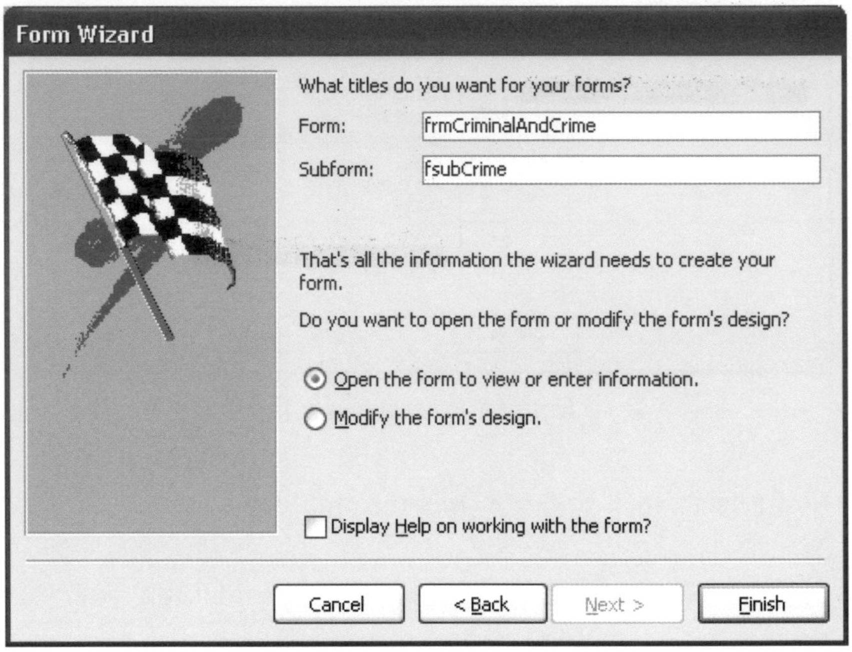

Figure 5.4: Saving the forms

Click Finish.

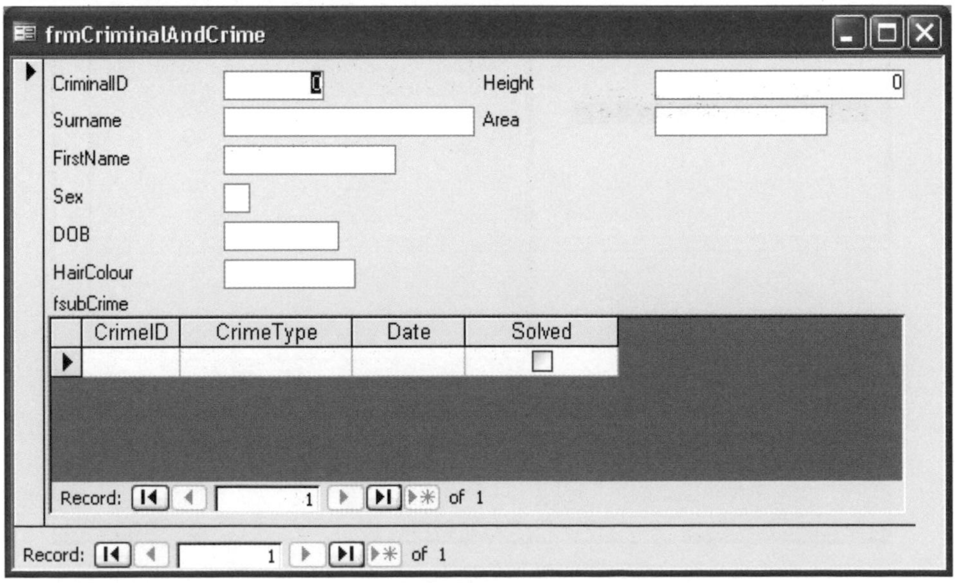

Figure 5.5

Editing the form

Now that you've created the form, there are a few things you need to do to make it look a bit more professional and user-friendly.

 Click the Design View icon.

 First, delete the label that says fsubCrime: Click on it and then press the Delete key.

Notice that the space given for the subform is much larger than it needs to be. Adjusting this so that it ends at the end of the Solved field takes a bit of trial and error!

 Click anywhere in the subform. Notice the small black or grey squares that now appear around it. Click and drag these squares to make the box narrower, but make sure the subform is deep enough to see the fields in the Detail section under the Form Header.

 Return to Form View to see if it's the right size – adjust this until you are happy with how it looks.

CriminalID		Height		0
Surname		Area		
FirstName				
Sex				
DOB				
HairColour				

CrimeID	CrimeType	Date	Solved
			☐

Record: ◄ ◄ 1 ► ►► ►* of 1

Record: ◄ ◄ 1 ► ►► ►* of 1

Figure 5.6

Combo Box

It will be convenient to make the CrimeID field a combo box.

 In Design View, click the Combo Box icon and drag out a field in the Detail section on the subform (not the main form).

 Select the option I want the combo box to look up the values in a table or query. Click Next.

Select tblCrime in the next window. Click Next.

 Select CrimeID, CrimeType, Date, and Solved from the Available Fields. Click Next.

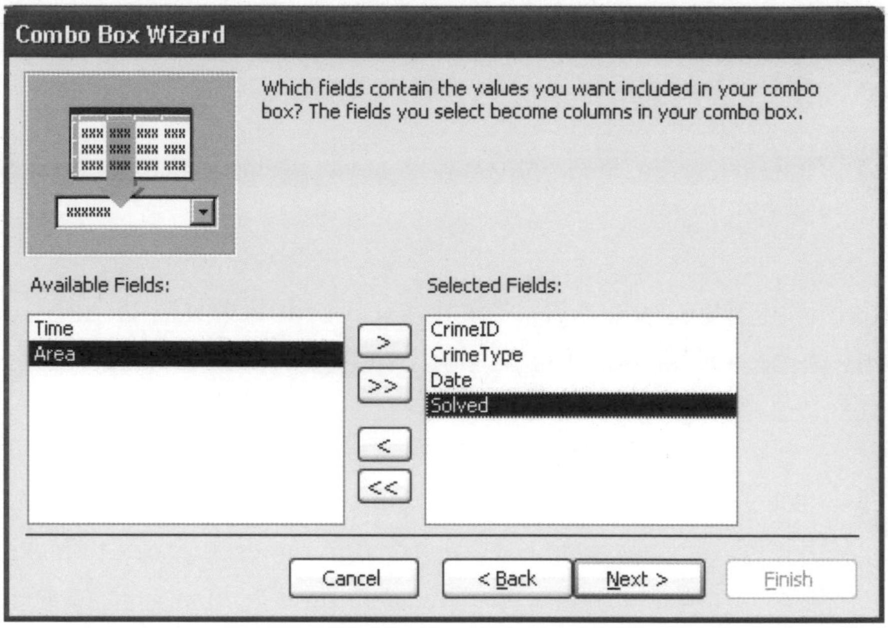

Combo Box Wizard

Which fields contain the values you want included in your combo box? The fields you select become columns in your combo box.

Available Fields:
```
Time
Area
```

Selected Fields:
```
CrimeID
CrimeType
Date
Solved
```

[>] [>>] [<] [<<]

Cancel | < Back | Next > | Finish

Figure 5.7

In Access 2003 you are now asked whether you want to sort the list. We'll leave it unsorted, so just click Next.

 Deselect the check box marked Hide key column and click Next.

 Select CrimeID from the next window. Click Next.

 Select Store that value in this field: and choose CrimeID from the drop-down list. Click Next.

 Save the combo box as CrimeID and click Finish.

Now look at the form in Form View. Notice that the original CrimeID field is still there, and the new one has been put right at the end. The original field needs to be deleted and the new one put in its place.

 In Design View, click the original CrimeID field to select it and press the Delete key.

 Right-click the new field and select Properties from the menu.

Make sure the All tab is selected in the Properties box, and change the Name field from Combo8 to CrimeID.

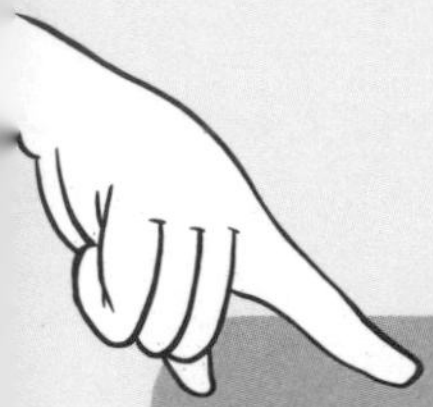

Combo Box: Combo8

| Combo8 | ⌄ |

| Format | Data | Event | Other | All |

```
Name . . . . . . . . . . . . . . . . . CrimeID
Control Source . . . . . . . . . . . CrimeID
Format . . . . . . . . . . . . . . . . .
Decimal Places . . . . . . . . . . . Auto
Input Mask . . . . . . . . . . . . . .
Row Source Type . . . . . . . . . Table/Query
Row Source . . . . . . . . . . . . . SELECT [tblCrime].[C
Column Count . . . . . . . . . . . . 4
Column Heads . . . . . . . . . . . No
Column Widths . . . . . . . . . . 2.54cm;2.54cm;2.54
```

Figure 5.8

 Go to Form View.

Now we'll change the position of the CrimeID field to be where the original was.

 Hold the mouse over the CrimeID label. Notice that the mouse pointer becomes a down arrow. Click the label, so that the whole column is highlighted.

 Now click and drag the label over to the left of the CrimeType field, and drop it.

The field should now be on the far left.

frmCriminalAndCrime

CriminalID	0		Height		0
Surname			Area		
FirstName					
Sex					
DOB					
HairColour					

CrimeID	CrimeType	Date	Solved
			☐

Record: ◄◄ ◄ 1 ► ►► ►✳ of 1

Record: ◄◄ ◄ 1 ► ►► ►✳ of 1

Figure 5.9

 Save the form.

Tab Order

Before starting the data entry, just make sure that the Tab Order is the way you like it on both forms. If not, go to the View menu whilst in Design View, and click Tab Order.

You may find that some of the fields are now called something like List18. You can change this by right-clicking on the field in Design View and changing the name in the Properties box.

Data Entry

OK, you've got your two forms up and running – it's time to enter some test data!

First enter the crimes:

 Open frmCrime from the Database window.

 Enter the crimes listed in Table 5.10.

CrimeID	CrimeType	Date	Time	Area	Solved
101	Vandalism	3/6/2000	08:00	Bottsworth	N
108	Counterfeit Money	1/6/2001	15:35	Runden	Y
102	Joy Riding	1/12/2000	14:20	Runden	N
111	Joy Riding	3/7/2001	10:55	Gullyford	Y
104	Littering	28/5/2001	13:15	Rinehead	N
112	Littering	14/7/2001	17:40	Rinehead	Y
105	Joy Riding	10/10/2000	04:10	Gullyford	N
106	Littering	19/7/2001	21:50	Rinehead	Y
107	Vandalism	28/7/2001	23:45	Hebbsfield	Y
109	Joy Riding	5/4/2001	22:10	Bottsworth	Y
103	Counterfeit Money	19/1/2001	15:05	Hebbsfield	N
110	Vandalism	16/2/2001	08:15	Rinehead	Y
113	Vandalism	25/4/2001	16:40	Hebbsfield	Y

Table 5.10

Tip:

You can use your **Log New Crime** button instead of the record selectors to go to a new record. Or, tabbing out of the last field will automatically take you to a new record.

When you have entered all the crimes, close frmCrime.

Now we will use the frmCriminalAndCrime form to enter a list of known criminals and the crimes they have committed.

 Open frmCriminalAndCrime.

 Enter the first criminal from Table 5.11, Sharon Hart, along with her personal details.

Now look at the last column in the table which lists the CrimeIDs of the crimes she has committed.

 Click in the CrimeID field in the subform. Select the row with CrimeID 107 from the list that appears.

Notice that the other crime details are automatically filled in.

 Repeat this for the second crime, CrimeID 110.

CriminalID	Surname	Firstname	Sex	DOB	Haircolour	Height	Area	CrimeIDs of Crimes Committed
201	Hart	Sharon	F	15/2/1979	Blonde	1.7	Bottsworth	107, 110
202	Hodson	Tony	M	2/9/1979	Light Brown	1.8	Bottsworth	110
203	Stevenson	Mike	M	25/6/1987	Black	1.7	Hebbsfield	108
204	Jones	Gareth	M	20/12/1984	Ginger	1.8	Gullyford	108
205	Hainsworth	John	M	12/4/1985	Ginger	1.7	Runden	113
206	Chisholm	Pete	M	14/8/1990	Light Brown	1.8	Hebbsfield	109, 111
207	Whitehead	Mel	F	28/5/1957	Light Brown	1.6	Rinehead	111
208	Goldsmith	Anne	F	3/10/1975	Dark Brown	1.6	Bottsworth	106

Table 5.11

 Enter all the other criminals from Table 5.11.

Try entering something other than M or F in the Sex field. What happens?

 When all the data has been entered, close the form.

Chapter 6

Queries

We will design some queries that will help find criminals who may have committed certain crimes.

For example, we could search for:

 All criminals who fit a certain witness description such as ginger hair, mid 20s, about 1.7m tall.

 All criminals who are known for committing certain types of crimes, and who work in certain areas.

We will make a query which allows us to search for criminals who fit a certain description.

New query

 Open the CrimeDatabase and click to select the Queries tab in the Database window.

 Either double-click Create query in Design view or click New, then Design View. Click OK.

Figure 6.1: The Show Table window

Select tblCriminal and click Add.

 Click Close.

 We want all the fields to appear in the query, so double-click each one in turn, and watch as they appear in the query grid below.

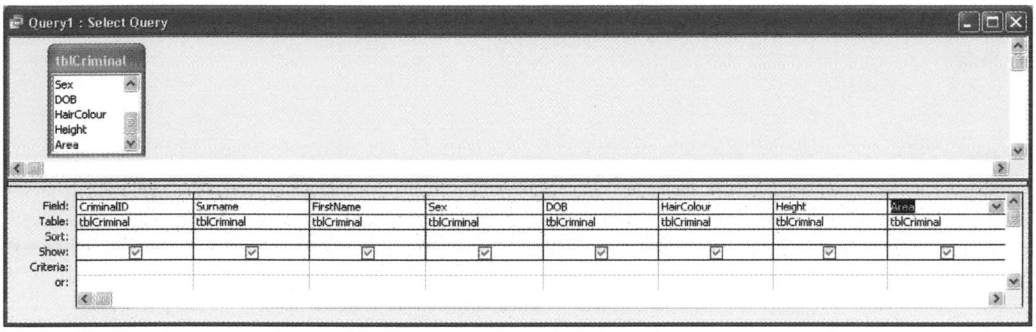

Figure 6.2: The query grid

Adding criteria

We would like the query to give a list of every criminal with light brown hair.

 In the Criteria row of the HairColour column, type Light Brown.

 Test the query by clicking the Run button. ────────────────

Your query results table should look like Figure 6.3.

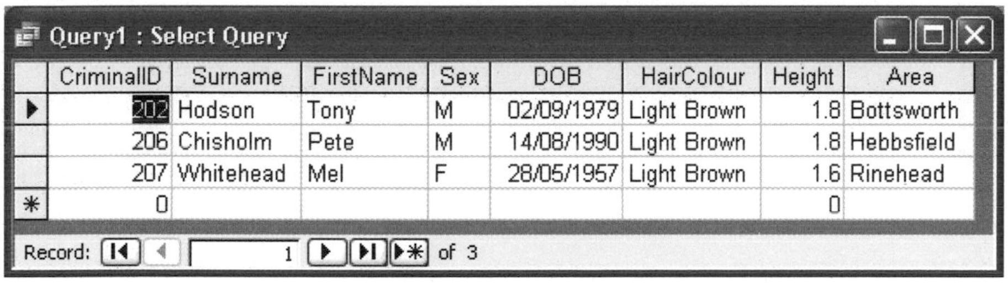

	CriminalID	Surname	FirstName	Sex	DOB	HairColour	Height	Area
▶	202	Hodson	Tony	M	02/09/1979	Light Brown	1.8	Bottsworth
	206	Chisholm	Pete	M	14/08/1990	Light Brown	1.8	Hebbsfield
	207	Whitehead	Mel	F	28/05/1957	Light Brown	1.6	Rinehead
*	0						0	

Record: 1 of 3

Figure 6.3: Query results

First row should be selected

 Save the query as qryHairColour, but don't close it.

We are now going to use this query as the basis for another query.

 Select File, Save As from the Menu bar.

 Enter qrySurname as the filename for the new query and click OK.

You will see qrySurname displayed in the Title bar.

Using wildcards

The character * in a criterion stands for any combination of characters. If you enter Ha* as the criterion for Surname, Access will find Hart and Hainsworth.

 In Design View delete the criterion Light Brown in the HairColour column.

 Enter the criterion H* in the criteria row in the Surname column. (See Figure 6.4.)

Selecting which fields to show

Sometimes you don't want every field to appear in the query results table. You can select which columns you want to appear.

 Click in the Show box in all the columns except Surname, Firstname, Sex and DOB to leave only these columns selected.

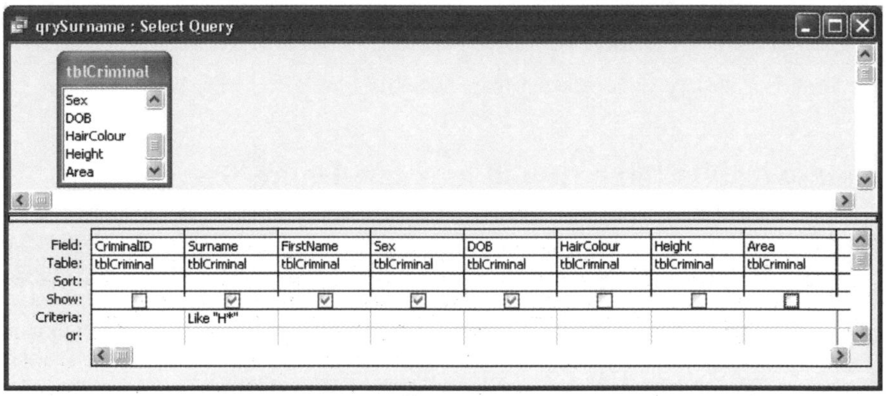

Figure 6.4: Using a wildcard

The query results table should list just the people with surnames beginning with H.

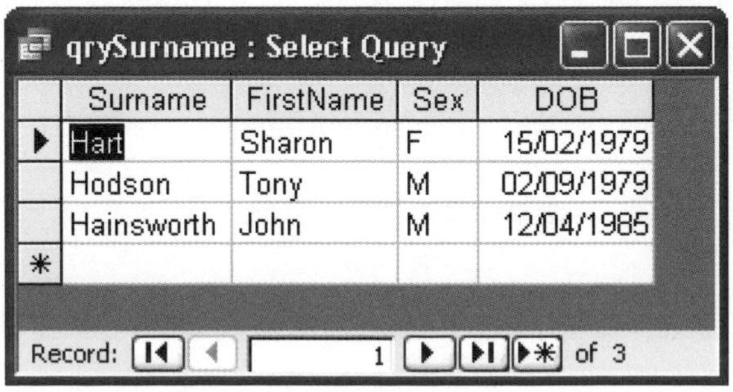

Figure 6.5: The Query results table

 Save the query. It should already be named qrySurname.

Sorting the query results

Suppose you want the results sorted in order of surname.

 In Design View, click in the Sort row of the Surname column, and select Ascending from the drop-down list.

 Test the results – the records should be listed in alphabetical order of surname.

If you wanted to sort on FirstName as well, so that Ann Hardy would always appear before Jill Hardy, for example, you could specify Ascending in the Sort row of FirstName as well. The sort criteria are read from left to right, so that records are first sorted on Surname, and then if there are two surnames the same, the records are sorted in order of FirstName.

If you wanted to sort in a different sequence, you can do so by moving the columns so that they appear in the order that you want to sort.

Suppose we want to have all the males appearing in alphabetical order, followed by all the females in alphabetical order.

 Switch to Design View.

 Select the Sex column by clicking in its column header. Then click anywhere in the selected column and move the column to the left of the Surname field.

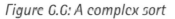 Specify a Descending Sort on the Sex field, and an Ascending Sort on the Surname and Firstname fields. Remove the criteria Like H* from the Surname column.

Field:	CriminalID	Sex	Surname	FirstName	DOB	HairColour	Height	Area
Table:	tblCriminal	tblCriminal	tblCriminal	tblCriminal	tblCriminal	tblCriminal	tblCriminal	tblCriminal
Sort:		Descending	Ascending	Ascending				
Show:	☐	☑	☑	☑	☑	☐	☐	☐
Criteria:								
or:								

Figure 6.6: A complex sort

Run the query. You should see the records in the following sequence:

qrySurname : Select Query

	Sex	Surname	FirstName	DOB
▶	M	Chisholm	Pete	14/08/1990
	M	Hainsworth	John	12/04/1985
	M	Hodson	Tony	02/09/1979
	M	Jones	Gareth	20/12/1984
	M	Stevenson	Mike	25/06/1987
	F	Goldsmith	Anne	03/10/1975
	F	Hart	Sharon	15/02/1979
	F	Whitehead	Mel	28/05/1957

Figure 6.7: Results of sorting

Using operators such as >, <

Suppose you want to find all the people in the database born after a certain date, say 01/01/1978.

 Return to Design View. In the criteria row for DOB, enter >01/01/1978.

 Run the query. Does it work?

Notice that you have to be careful whether or not you want to include people born on 01/01/1978.

 Try changing the criteria to >02/09/1979.

 Run the query.

Tony Hodson will not appear in the results table. If you want to include people born on that day, you must write >=02/09/1979.

 Try this now, and run the query again.

If you want to find all people born before 02/09/1979, enter <02/09/1979 as the criteria.

Suppose you want to find all people of approximately a certain height.

 If Height is not on the query grid, double-click it to put it at the end.

 Delete all existing criteria.

 In the criteria row under Height, enter Between 1.6 and 1.7.

Run the query again and check the results.

Multiple criteria

Suppose you wanted to find only males between 1.6m and 1.7m in height. In words, you would write the criteria as

(Sex = 'M') AND (Height between 1.6 and 1.7)
or something similar.

In an Access query, if you put more than one criteria on the same line, it assumes you want both.

 In the criteria row under Sex, enter M.

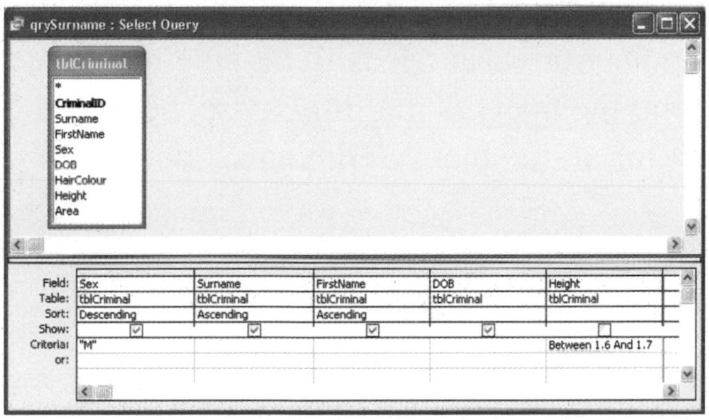

 Figure 6.8: Specifying multiple criteria

Run the query and check your results. Hainsworth and Stevenson should be shown.

Using OR in criteria

Now suppose you wanted to find all people from Rinehead OR Gullyford. The criteria have to be written on different lines.

 Return to Design View. If Area is not shown in the query grid, add it by double-clicking it.

 Delete any existing criteria and enter new criteria as shown below:

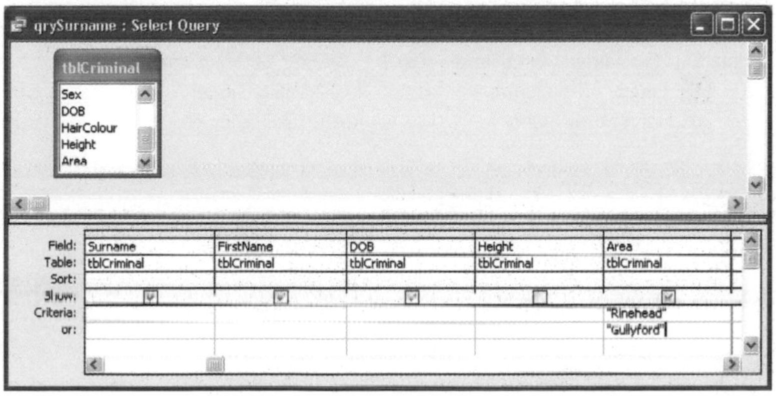

Figure 6.9: Specifying "OR" in criteria

Tip:
Access automatically adds the quote marks to the criteria, so you don't need to type them.

Run the query and check your results. Jones and Whitehead should be displayed.

 Save and close the query.

Allowing the user to enter criteria

Look back at the first query you created at the start of this chapter. It found all the people with light brown hair.

Since the criminal description the user is looking for will be constantly changing, the user needs to be able to re-enter the criteria each time the query is run (otherwise we would need one query to search for all the blonde criminals, another for ginger, etc).

From the Database window select the Queries tab and open qryHairColour. Make sure you are in Design View.

From the File menu, select Save As and save this query as qryWitnessDescription.

In the Criteria row in the HairColour column delete Light Brown and enter [Please enter hair colour].

To show what this does, we'll run the query quickly:

 Click the Run button on the menu bar.

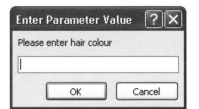

Figure 6.10: Enter Parameter Value

 Enter Ginger and press OK.

	CriminalID	Surname	FirstName	Sex	DOB	HairColour	Height	Area
▶	204	Jones	Gareth	M	20/12/1984	Ginger	1.8	Gullyford
	205	Hainsworth	John	M	12/04/1985	Ginger	1.7	Runden
✱	0						0	

Record: ◄◄ ◄ 1 ► ►► ►✱ of 2

Figure 6.11: Query results

Two records should be returned from the query as shown in Figure 6.11.

Return to the query design by pressing the Design View icon.

Tip:
You need to type the square brackets too!

Tip:
The text you write in square brackets is what appears in this window! This will work in any query.

We can now do the same for the height, but this time we really need to enter a height range.

- Enter Between [Enter lowest height] And [Enter highest height] in the Criteria row of the Height column.
- Run the query again to check it works, entering sensible values for the Height and HairColour.
- Save and close the query.

Queries with more than one table

In order to look up criminals who have committed certain types of crimes, the query will have to involve all three tables.

- Start a new query by clicking New in the Database window. Select Design View and click OK.
- Add all three tables by selecting them and clicking Add.
- Click Close.
- Add the field CriminalID from tblSolvedCrimes.
- Add the fields Surname and Firstname from tblCriminal.
- Add the field CrimeType from tblCrime.

Figure 6.12

Tip:
Make sure the **Queries** tab is selected before you click **New**!

Tip:
Although you could choose **CriminalID** from **tblCriminal**, it is important to select it from the correct table. Make sure it is from **tblSolvedCrimes**.

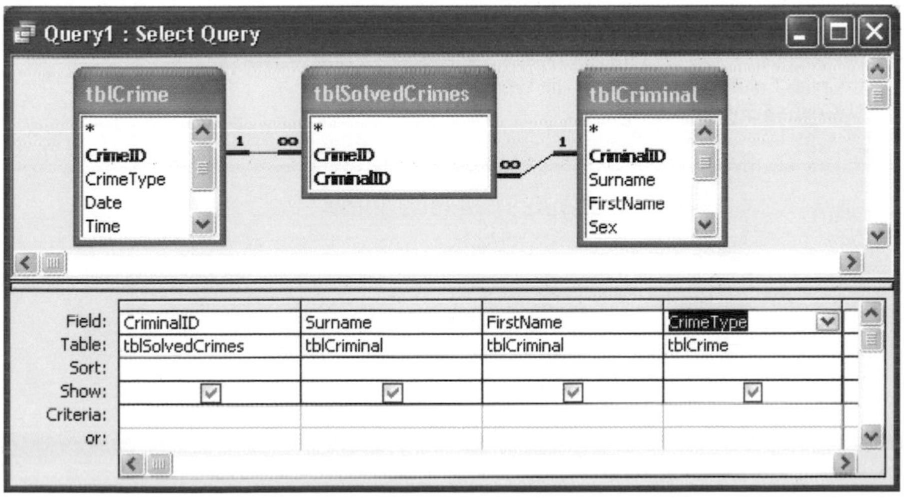

 Type [Enter crime type] as the criterea in the CrimeType column.

We'd like the results sorted by Surname, so select Ascending from the drop-down list in the Sort row of the Surname column.

Run the query by clicking the Run button.

Enter Vandalism as the crime type.

Query1 : Select Query

	CriminalID	Surname	FirstName	CrimeType
▶	205	Hainsworth	John	Vandalism
	201	Hart	Sharon	Vandalism
	201	Hart	Sharon	Vandalism
	202	Hodson	Tony	Vandalism
*				

Record: |◄| |◄| 1 |►| |►|| |►*| of 4

Figure 6.13

Notice that Sharon Hart's record appears twice – we don't want this. To make sure no record appears twice just follow the instructions below:

 In the View menu, click the down arrow and select SQL View.

☒	Design View
▦	Datasheet View
SQL	SQL View

 Don't panic! This code looks complicated but you don't need to understand any of it. In the first line, add the word DISTINCT after SELECT, so that it looks like Figure 6.8.

Query1 : Select Query

```
SELECT DISTINCT tblSolvedCrimes.CriminalID, tblCriminal.Surname, tblCriminal.FirstName,
tblCrime.CrimeType
FROM tblCriminal INNER JOIN (tblCrime INNER JOIN tblSolvedCrimes ON tblCrime.CrimeID =
tblSolvedCrimes.CrimeID) ON tblCriminal.CriminalID = tblSolvedCrimes.CriminalID
WHERE (((tblCrime.CrimeType)=[Enter crime type]))
ORDER BY tblCriminal.Surname;
```

Figure 6.14: SQL View

Tip:

SQL stands for **Structured Query Language**. It is a simplified programming language used for querying databases.

▷ Now run the query again to check that it has worked.

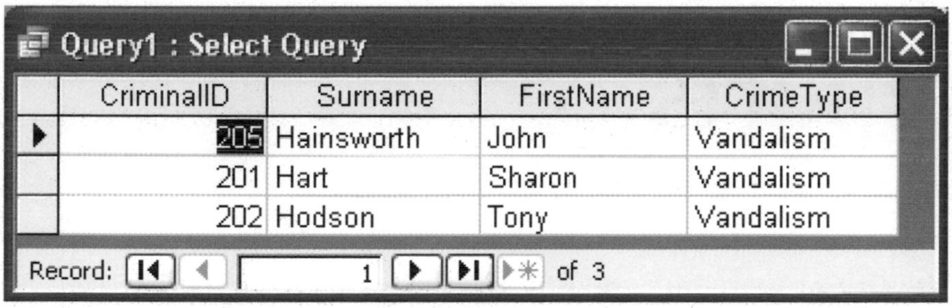

CriminalID	Surname	FirstName	CrimeType
▶	205	Hainsworth	John	Vandalism
	201	Hart	Sharon	Vandalism
	202	Hodson	Tony	Vandalism

Query1 : Select Query

Record: |◀| |◀| 1 |▶| |▶|| |▶*| of 3

Figure 6.15

▷ Save the query as qryCrimeType and click the Close button. ———————

Reports

Reports are useful for presenting query results in a more professional way, but they also have other useful features. You can display Sum or Average fields in a report, or do almost any other arithmetic operation on numeric fields.

We will use the Count function to give a summary of how many crimes were committed in each month during a specified period.

First of all, we need to create a query that will select all the crimes in a specified period.

Creating the basic query

 In the Database window, select the Queries tab and click New.

 Make sure Design View is selected and click OK.

 Select tblCrime and click Add.

▶ This query will only include this table, so now close this window by clicking the Close button.

▶ Double-click the fields CrimeType and Date.

They should appear in the query grid as shown in Figure 7.1:

Figure 7.1

Type Between [Enter start date] And [Enter end date] as the criteria in the Date column.

 Run the query to check that it works. ───────────────────

 Save the query as qryCrimesInPeriod and close the query.

Creating the Report

Tip:
"Enter start date" and "Enter end date" are field names which will be used on the report.

The report will be based on the query we have just created, qryCrimesInPeriod.

 In the Database window click the Reports tab, then click New.

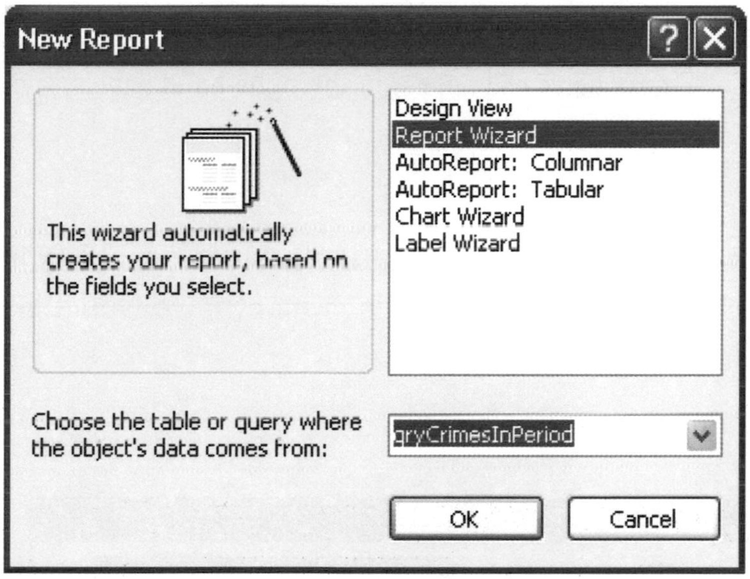

New Report [?][X]

This wizard automatically creates your report, based on the fields you select.

Design View
Report Wizard
AutoReport: Columnar
AutoReport: Tabular
Chart Wizard
Label Wizard

Choose the table or query where the object's data comes from: qryCrimesInPeriod

OK   Cancel

Figure 7.2

 Select Report Wizard from the list of options, and choose qryCrimesInPeriod from the drop-down list.

Click OK. The following window appears:

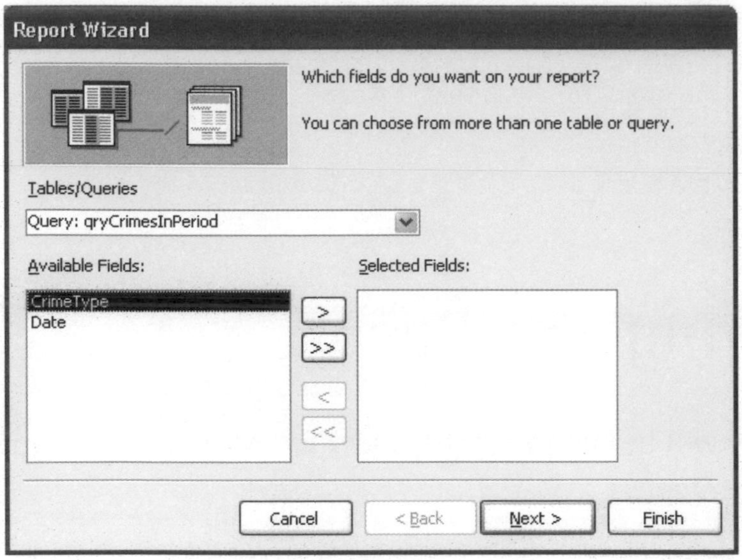

Figure 7.3: Report Wizard

 We would like both CrimeType and Date to appear on the report so click >>. These fields will appear in the right-hand pane.

 Click Next.

You are now asked to add grouping levels. Since we would like to see which crimes were committed each month, we would like Date to be the first grouping level.

> Select Date and click >.

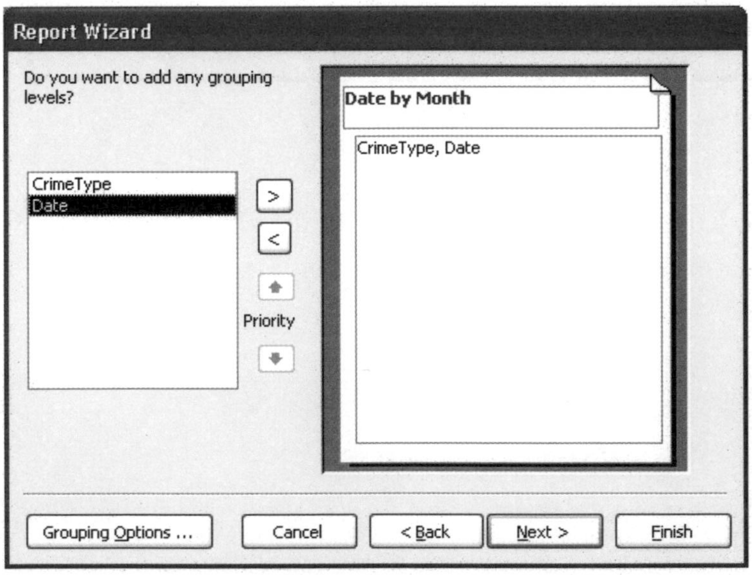

Figure 7.4: Grouping levels

 Click Next. Select CrimeType from the first drop-down list to sort the records by CrimeType and click Next.

The next two windows ask about the format of the report. You can try out some different styles, otherwise just click Next in each window.

 Save the report as rptCrimesInPeriod and click Finish.

You are now asked for the start and end date of the report.

 Enter 1/1/2001 and 1/1/2002 as the start and end dates.

rptCrimesInPeriod		
rptCrimesInPeriod		
Date by Month	*CrimeType*	*Date*
January 2001		
	Counterfeit Money	19/01/2001
February 2001		
	Vandalism	16/02/2001
April 2001		
	Joy Riding	05/04/2001
	Vandalism	25/04/2001
May 2001		
	Littering	28/05/2001
June 2001		
	Counterfeit Money	01/06/2001

Figure 7.5

You have now created the basic report! Now we need to add fields which count the number of crimes committed each month, and also add a total number of crimes over the selected period.

Counting the crimes

To do this we will add a field in the Date Header. When inserting fields that add up or do some other maths operation on a report, you have to be careful which section of the report the field is put in.

 Go to report design by clicking the Design View icon. ———————

 Click the Text Box icon in the Toolbox, and click once on the right hand side under the Date Header. ———————

 Click in the field where it says Unbound and type =Count(CrimeType).

The figure shows the rptCrimesInPeriod report in Design View, with report sections labelled.

rptCrimesInPeriod : Report

| Report Header |
| rptCrimesInPeriod |

| Page Header |
| Date by Month | CrimeType | Date |

| Date Header |
| =Format$([Date], "mmmm yy, | Text12: | =Count([CrimeType]) |

| Detail |
| CrimeType | Date |

| Page Footer |
| =Now() | ="Page " & [Page] & " of " & [Pages] |

| Report Footer |

These are the report sections

Figure 7.6: rptCrimesInPeriod in Design View

Now see if this works by clicking the Print Preview icon.

rptCrimesInPeriod

rptCrimesInPeriod

Date by Month	CrimeType	Date	
January 2001		Text12:	1
	Counterfeit Money	19/01/2001	
February 2001		Text12:	1
	Vandalism	16/02/2001	
April 2001		Text12:	2
	Joy Riding	05/04/2001	
	Vandalism	25/04/2001	
May 2001		Text12:	1
	Littering	28/05/2001	
June 2001		Text12:	1
	Counterfeit Money	01/06/2001	

Page: 1

Figure 7.7

That seems to work! Now we will add one more field to total all the crimes in the report, then we will do some tidying up.

Return to Design View.

To get a total for the whole report, we need to add a calculated field in the Report Footer. In fact, we can put in exactly the same expression we did before, but because it is in a different section on the report, it will give a different total.

Click on the field =Count([CrimeType]) that you created above, and click Copy on the Edit menu at the top of the screen.

Click on the bar named Report Footer, and click Paste from the Edit menu.

The same field should appear. Now we want to rename the labels and make sure the calculated fields appear in the right place.

 In Design View, change the labels of both the fields you have just created, and the report title, to look like Figure 7.8.

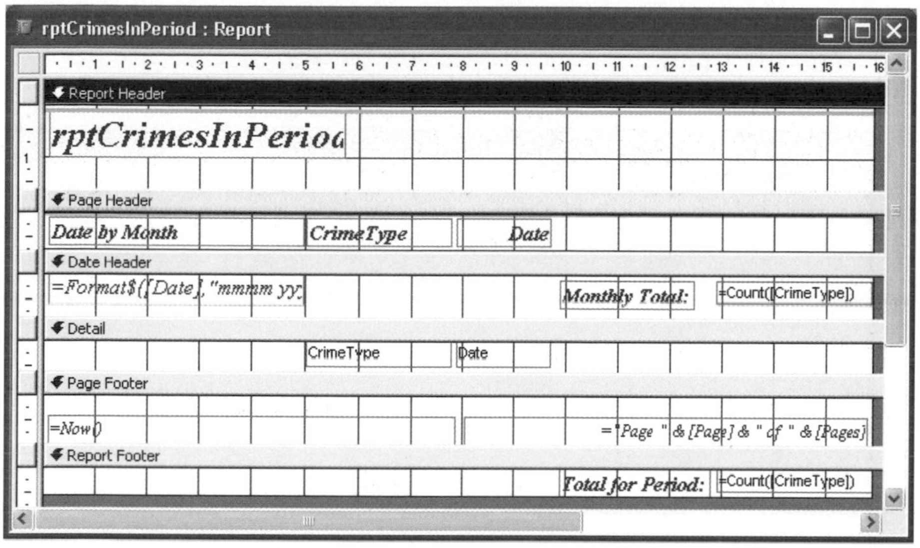

Figure 7.8

 Now test the report by clicking the Print Preview button. ——————————

Date Footer

Suppose you wanted the subtotals below each list of crimes instead of above them. You would do this by moving the Count field from the Date Header to the Date Footer. As there is no Date Footer on your report, the first step is to add this.

 Click the Sorting and Grouping button on the Report Design toolbar. ———

 The Sorting and Grouping window appears. In the Group Properties at the bottom of the window select Yes next to Group Footer.

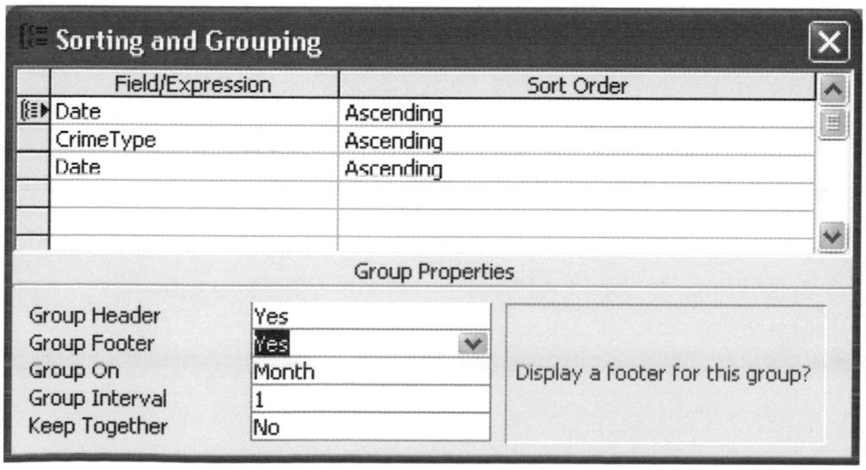

	Field/Expression	Sort Order	
	Date	Ascending	
	CrimeType	Ascending	
	Date	Ascending	

Group Properties

Group Header	Yes
Group Footer	Yes
Group On	Month
Group Interval	1
Keep Together	No

Display a footer for this group?

Figure 7.9: Sorting and Grouping window

Tip:
Anything in the Page footer appears at the bottom of every page in the report.

Close the window. You will notice that there is now a section labelled Date Footer on the report.

 Click and drag the Count field that is currently in the Date Header to the Date Footer.

 Run the report.

rptCrimesInPeriod				_ □ X
Date by Month	Crime Type	Date		
January 2001				
	Counterfeit Money	19/01/2001		
			Monthly Total:	1
February 2001				
	Vandalism	16/02/2001		
			Monthly Total:	1
April 2001				
	Joy Riding	05/04/2001		
	Vandalism	25/04/2001		
			Monthly Total:	2

Page: |◄ ◄   1   ► ►| ◄

Figure 7.10

Inserting the date in the title

It would be useful to have the selected date range appearing at the top of the report. We will insert it as follows:

 Go to Design View by clicking the Design View icon.

 Click the Text Box icon on the Toolbar and drag out a field in the Report Header.

Change the text in the Text Box from Unbound to [Enter start date].

Add a second text box to the right of the first, and enter the text [Enter end date].

Delete the first label and change the other to say to.

 Now change the fonts and rearrange the report to look like Figure 7.11.

The field name you write in the text box is the same as you wrote in square brackets in **qryCrimesInPeriod**.

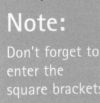

Note:

Don't forget to enter the square brackets too.

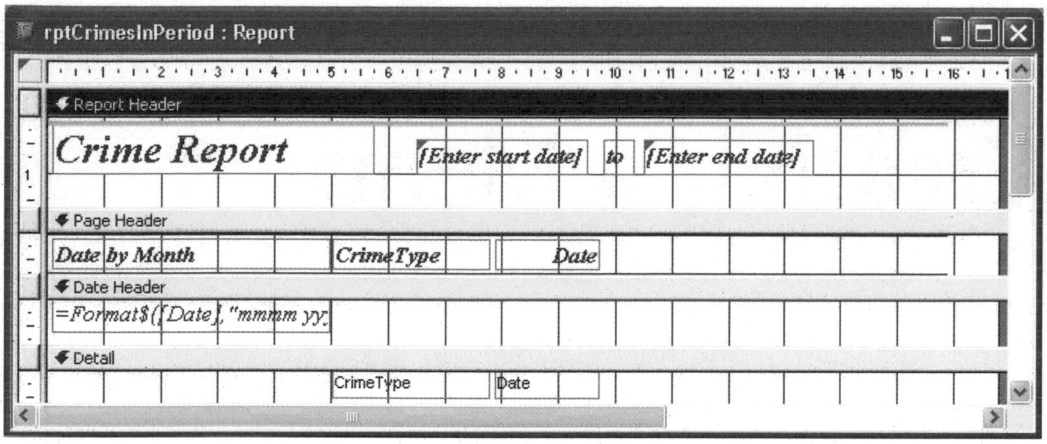

Figure 7.11

Tip:

When you run the report, the dates you enter should now appear in the Report Header. If they don't, go back and check that the text you have written on the report is exactly the same as the text you wrote in square brackets in **qryCrimesInPeriod**.

▶ Click the Print Preview icon to check that these fields work. ──────

▶ Save and close your report.

Exercise

It would be nice to have a report based on qryWitnessDescription which would print out names of possible suspects.

Try and create this report using the Report Wizard just as you did for the report above, saving it as rptWitnessDescription.

When you have created the report, edit the labels and move the fields around so that they look like Figure 7.12.

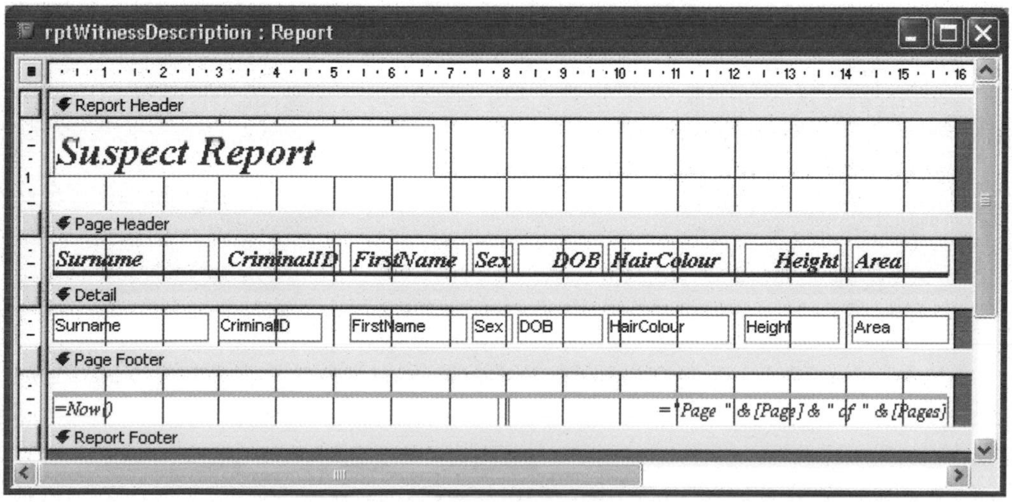

Figure 7.12

▶ Save and close your report – you will need it in the next chapter.

Creating a Menu

OK, this is the fun part. You've done the hard work creating forms and reports, and now you need to make the whole database a bit more user-friendly.

By creating a menu, you can hide from the user the inner workings of your database, such as the Database window.

Before creating the menu in Access, you need to plan out the menu structure.

Menu Structure

The basic menu structure we will develop is shown in Figure 8.1.

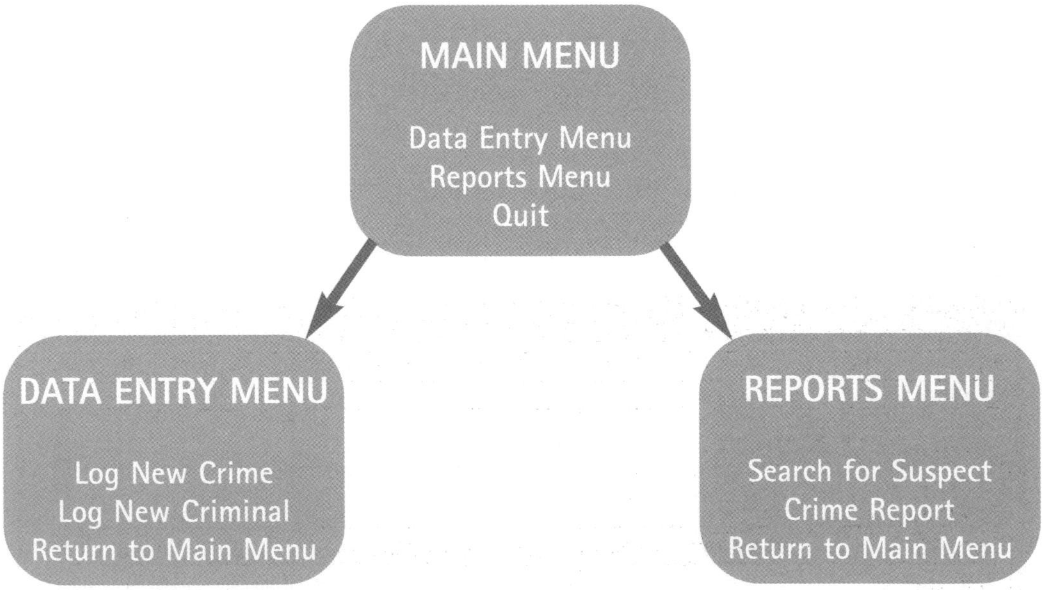

MAIN MENU

Data Entry Menu
Reports Menu
Quit

DATA ENTRY MENU

Log New Crime
Log New Criminal
Return to Main Menu

REPORTS MENU

Search for Suspect
Crime Report
Return to Main Menu

Figure 8.1

Switchboard Manager

The quickest way to create a menu in Access is to use the Switchboard Manager.

- Open the Switchboard Manager by clicking Tools, Database Utilities, Switchboard Manager.

Because you haven't created a switchboard yet, you will get the following message:

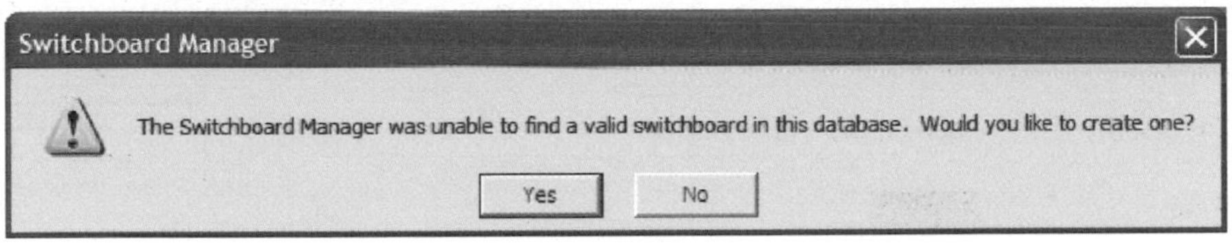

Figure 8.2

- Click Yes and the Switchboard Manager window opens.

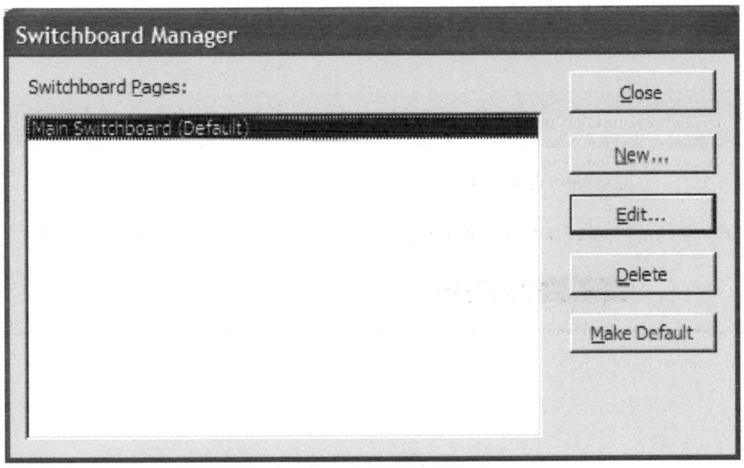

Figure 8.3

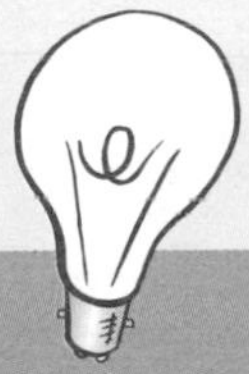

Tip:
Switchboard is the name Access gives to a menu screen.

It is easiest to start by creating the two submenus before the main menu, so first we will create the Data Entry Menu.

- Click New, and enter Data Entry Menu as the Switchboard Page Name. Click OK.
- Now edit this menu: select Data Entry Menu and click Edit.
- Click New, and the Edit Switchboard Item window appears.

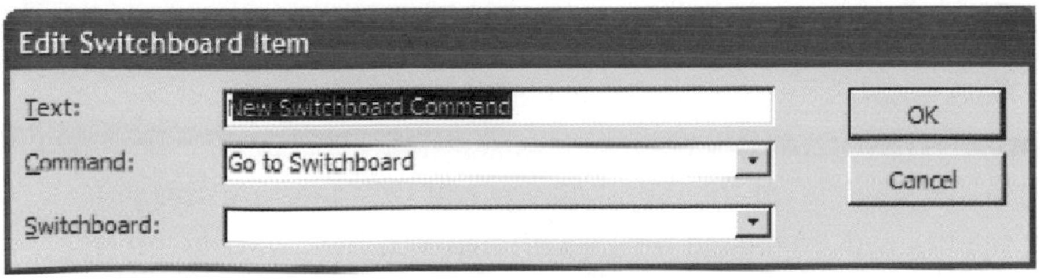

Figure 8.4

In this window you specify the text that appears next to the menu button, and the action that the button will perform. We want it to open the frmCrime form.

 Enter Log New Crime as the text.

 Select Open Form in Add Mode as the Command.

Select frmCrime as the form and click OK.

Edit Switchboard Item

Text:	Log New Crime		OK
Command:	Open Form in Add Mode	▾	Cancel
Form:	frmCrime	▾	

Figure 8.5

Create another menu item on the Data Entry Menu called Log New Criminal, which opens the frmCriminalAndCrime form.

Edit Switchboard Item

Text:	Log New Criminal		OK
Command:	Open Form in Add Mode	▾	Cancel
Form:	frmCriminalAndCrime	▾	

Figure 8.6

Navigating between menus

On every menu you must have a button to get back to the Main Menu – or you'll get stuck on one menu! You create this the same way as the Open Form buttons you created above, only this time the Command will be Go To Switchboard.

 Close the Edit Switchboard Page window.

 First of all, rename the Main Switchboard as Main Menu by selecting it and clicking Edit. Now change the name in the Switchboard Name field.

Click Close.

 Create an item on the Data Entry Menu called Return to Main Menu, with command Go To Switchboard. The Switchboard will be Main Menu.

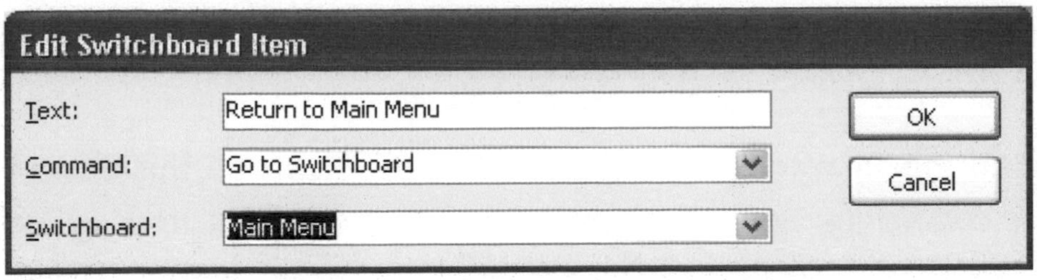

Edit Switchboard Item

Text:	Return to Main Menu	OK
Command:	Go to Switchboard	Cancel
Switchboard:	Main Menu	

Figure 8.7

Creating the Reports/Queries Menu

Now try and create the Reports Menu in the same way that you did the Data Entry Menu.

The Search for Suspect item should open report rptWitnessDescription.

The Crime Report should open rptCrimesInPeriod.

There must also be an item named Return to Main Menu.

The **Reports** menu has 3 items on it.

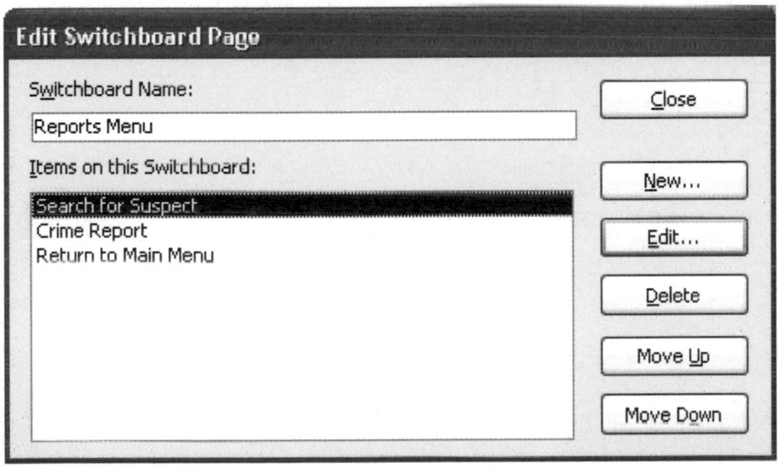

Edit Switchboard Page

Switchboard Name:

Reports Menu

Items on this Switchboard:

Search for Suspect
Crime Report
Return to Main Menu

Close
New...
Edit...
Delete
Move Up
Move Down

Figure 8.8

Make sure all the menu items have the right names, then return to the Switchboard Manager window.

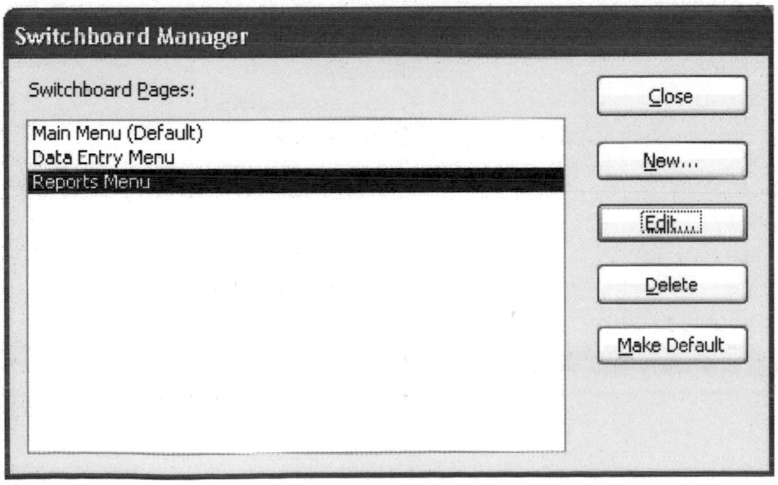

Switchboard Manager

Switchboard Pages:

Main Menu (Default)
Data Entry Menu
Reports Menu

Close
New...
Edit...
Delete
Make Default

Figure 8.9

Creating the Main Menu

You do this in exactly the same way. All the items on this menu will have commands Go To Switchboard, except the Quit item which will specify Exit Application.

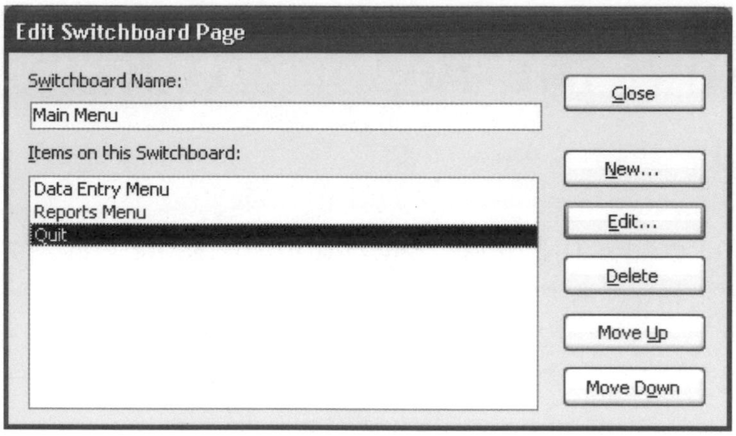

Figure 8.10

When you have created the menu, close the Switchboard Manager by clicking Close.

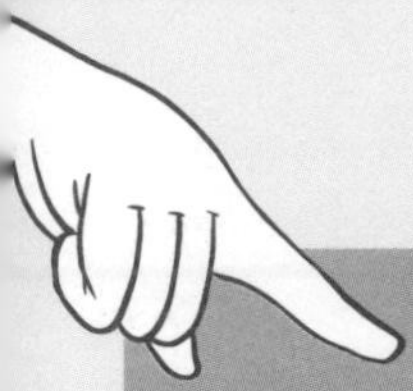

Tip:
Don't forget to add a heading to each of your menus, e.g. **Data Entry Menu**.

Startup options

Now you have a menu, it would make sense to make it appear automatically when you load the CrimeDatabase. You can do this by editing the Startup options.

- Click Tools, Startup.
- Enter CrimeDatabase as the Application Title.
- Select Switchboard from the drop-down list under Display Form/Page.

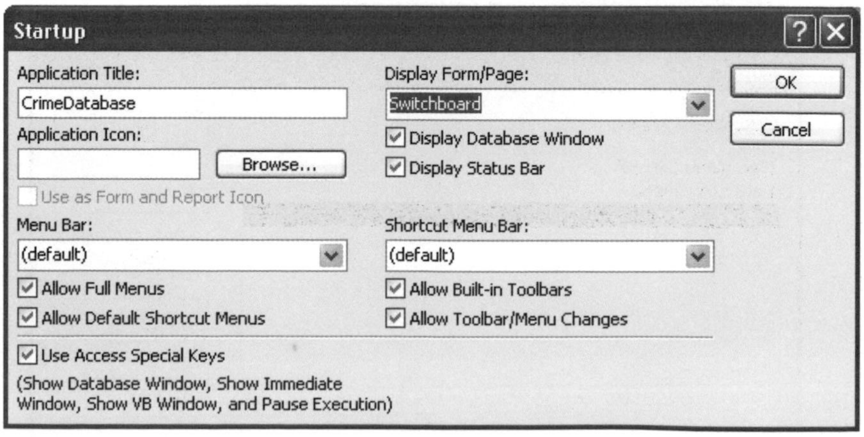

Figure 8.11

- Click OK.

Testing

If you are doing a course that involves producing a database, you will be required to show that you have tested your system thoroughly, and that it does what it is supposed to do. This will involve two stages:

1. Draw up a test plan with test data to test every menu, form, query and report in your system. The test plan should specify the purpose of each test and what the expected result is.

2. Carry out each test and take a screenshot of the result, or print out a report if that is what you are testing, to include in your documentation.

Here is part of a sample test plan:

Test	Purpose of test	Test data/Method	Expected result
1	Make sure the menu appears automatically when the database is opened	Open the database	Menu appears automatically
2	Test that button works correctly	Click Data Entry button on main menu	Data Entry menu appears
3	Test option to log new crime	Click Log new crime button	Blank screen appears ready to enter new crime
4	Test data entry from to log new crime	Enter CrimeID 257, Joy Riding, 03/10/2002, Bottsworth	Record accepted
5	Test validation on Sex field in Criminal form	Click Log new Criminal on Data Entry menu and enter H in Sex field	Error message displayed
6	(etc)		
7			

Figure 8.12: Sample test plan

Presenting Test results

As you carry out each test, take a screenshot of the result by pressing Alt and Prt Scr together. This copies an image of the screen into memory, from where it can be pasted into your Word document. You can crop the image to show just the part of the screen you want.

Annotate your test results by hand to highlight any points that are noteworthy.

For example:

Here are the test results.

Test 1 (Test opening menu)

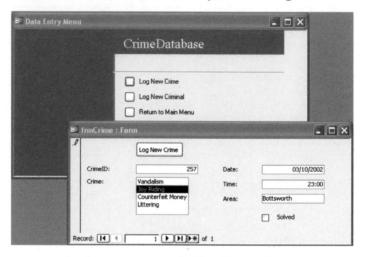

The menu appeared as expected.

Tests 2-4 (Test Data Entry menu option to log new crime)

These tests worked as expected. The Data Entry menu appeared and when Log New Crime was chosen, a blank screen appeared for data to be entered.

Test 5 (Test validation)

An error message was displayed when an invalid entry was made in the Sex field.

Evaluation of the system

You should check carefully what documentation you have to provide with your completed database. You will probably be required to evaluate the system. If you have a real user, let them test your system, and find any areas that they would like to see improved. Maybe they will write a letter that you can include in your documentation.

Try and be self-critical and note where improvements could be made to your system. You are not expected to get it perfect on your first try!

Index